Charlotte's Web

Contents

원서 읽는 단어장 소개 6
이 책의 구성 8
이 책의 활용법 10
전문가가 알려주는 원서 읽기 Tip 12

1. Before Breakfast
Let's walk in the Book 16
Vocabulary in Charlotte's Web 18

2. Wilbur
Let's walk in the Book 24
Vocabulary in Charlotte's Web 26

3. Escape
Let's walk in the Book 30
Vocabulary in Charlotte's Web 32

4. Loneliness
Let's walk in the Book 42
Vocabulary in Charlotte's Web 44

5. Charlotte
Let's walk in the Book 52
Vocabulary in Charlotte's Web 54

6. Summer Days
Let's walk in the Book 64
Vocabulary in Charlotte's Web 66

7. Bad News
Let's walk in the Book 72
Vocabulary in Charlotte's Web 74

8. A Talk at Home
Let's walk in the Book 76
Vocabulary in Charlotte's Web 78

9. Wilbur's Boast
Let's walk in the Book 80
Vocabulary in Charlotte's Web 82

10. An Explosion
Let's walk in the Book 90
Vocabulary in Charlotte's Web 92

11. The Miracle
Let's walk in the Book 100
Vocabulary in Charlotte's Web 102

12. A Meeting
   Let's walk in the Book · 106
   Vocabulary in Charlotte's Web · 108

13. Good Progress
   Let's walk in the Book · 112
   Vocabulary in Charlotte's Web · 114

14. Dr. Dorian
   Let's walk in the Book · 122
   Vocabulary in Charlotte's Web · 124

15. The Crickets
   Let's walk in the Book · 128
   Vocabulary in Charlotte's Web · 130

16. Off to the Fair
   Let's walk in the Book · 132
   Vocabulary in Charlotte's Web · 134

17. Uncle
   Let's walk in the Book · 142
   Vocabulary in Charlotte's Web · 144

18. The Cool of the Evening

   Let's walk in the Book · 148

   Vocabulary in Charlotte's Web · 150

19. The Egg Sac

   Let's walk in the Book · 154

   Vocabulary in Charlotte's Web · 156

20. The hour of Triumph

   Let's walk in the Book · 162

   Vocabulary in Charlotte's Web · 164

21. Last Days

   Let's walk in the Book · 170

   Vocabulary in Charlotte's Web · 172

22. A Warm Wind

   Let's walk in the Book · 178

   Vocabulary in Charlotte's Web · 180

   Answers · 188

   Index · 190

   영어원서 읽기 Tips · 201

원서 읽는 단어장 소개

누구나 추천하는 최고의 영어 공부법, 영어원서 읽기!

　최근 영어원서 읽기가 영어 공부법으로 주목받고 있습니다. 영어를 많이 접하는 것이 영어 실력을 향상시키는 가장 바람직한 방법이라는 공감대가 형성되면서, 쉽고 저렴하게 영어를 접할 수 있는 '원서 읽기'가 그 대안으로 각광받고 있는 것이지요.

　실제로도 영어 좀 한다는 사람들이 원서 읽기를 추천하거나, 어린 아이들이 엄마표 영어연수 등을 통해 원서를 읽는 많은 사례들을 인터넷 상에서 쉽게 찾아볼 수 있습니다.

남녀노소 모두에게 사랑받는 Charlotte's Web을 영어원서로 읽어보자!

　이 책은 미국의 작가 E. B. White가 1952년에 출간한 아동 소설입니다. 잔잔하고 감동적인 이야기로 아동 문학의 고전으로 인정받고 있으며, 아이들뿐 아니라 어른들에게도 두루 읽혀지면서 출간된 지 50년이 지난 지금도 베스트셀러 목록에 올라있을 만큼 큰 사랑을 받고 있습니다. 그 명성에 걸맞게 많은 작품상을 수상하기도 했는데 특히 미국 최고 권위를 자랑하는 '뉴베리 아너 상'을 받기도 했습니다.

　한국에서도 번역서가 출간되어 꾸준한 사랑을 받고 있고, 원서에 사용된 어휘와 표현들도 매우 쉬운 편이어서 '가장 많이 읽혀지는 원서' 중의 한 권이기도 합니다.

　또 이 책은 70년대에 애니메이션으로 제작되었으며, 2006년에는 다코타 패닝 주연의 실사 영화로도 만들어졌습니다. 원서를 읽기 전, 후에 이 영화를 함께 보면 많은 도움을 얻을 수 있을 것입니다.

원서 읽기를 위한 최고의 친구, 『원서 읽는 단어장』!!

원서 읽기가 영어공부를 하는 좋은 수단이긴 하지만, 한 번쯤 원서를 읽어 본 독자들은 대부분 다음과 같은 고민을 하곤 합니다.

누가 여기 나오는 단어 좀 찾아주면 안 되나?
모르는 단어가 나올 때마다 사전을 찾을 수도 없고,
그렇다고 그냥 지나치자니 뭔가 찜찜한데...

지금 내가 제대로 읽고 이해하고 있는 걸까?
번역된 책을 찾아서 일일이 대조할 수도 없고,
뭔가 확인할 방법이 있었으면 좋겠는데...

이런 문제를 해결해주고자, 여기 『원서 읽는 단어장』이 왔습니다!
원서 읽는 단어장은, 영어원서에 나온 어려운 어휘들을 완벽히 정리해서 원서 읽기의 부담감을 줄이고 보다 효과적으로 영어실력을 쌓을 수 있도록 도와주는 책입니다. 또한 이해력을 점검하는 Comprehension Quiz를 통해 내가 원서를 정확히 읽고 있는지 확인해볼 수 있습니다.

『원서 읽는 단어장』 시리즈를 통해 영어원서를 보다 쉽고 재미있게 읽고, 영어실력도 쑥쑥 향상시켜보세요.

이 책은 E.B. White(이비 화이트)의 대표작 Charlotte's Web(샬롯의 거미줄) 독자들을 위해 만들어졌습니다. 위 영어원서는 시중 서점 및 인터넷 서점에서 쉽게 구입할 수 있습니다.

이 책의 구성

Let's walk in the Book

원서를 제대로 읽고 이해하고 있는지 측정해보는 간단한 퀴즈입니다.

원어민 Extensive Reading 전문가가 출제한 쉽고 재미있는 문제들로 구성되어 있습니다. 퀴즈를 풀어보고 틀린 부분이 있다면, 제대로 이해한 것이 맞는지 해당 내용을 다시 한 번 점검해봐야겠죠?

퀴즈는 각 챕터별로 약 5개 안팎의 문제가 출제되어 있습니다.

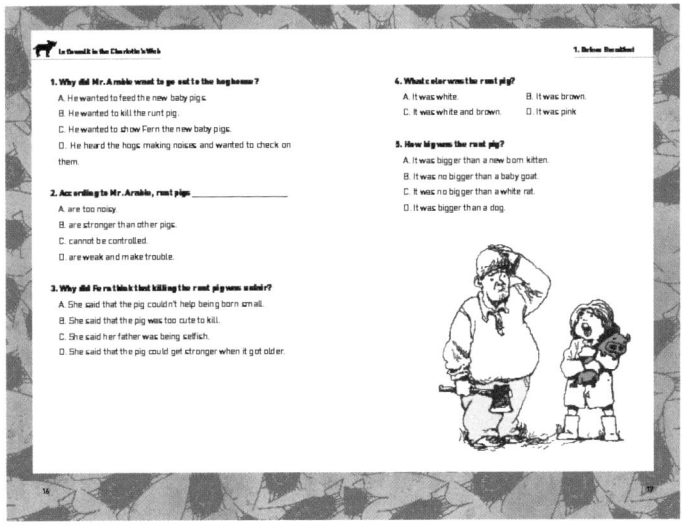

각 챕터를 읽고 바로 문제를 풀어보는 것도 좋고, 혹은 시간이 되는 대로 쭉 읽은 후 해당 부분만큼 문제를 풀어보는 것도 좋은 방법입니다. 자신의 상황과 스타일에 맞게 적절히 활용하세요!

정답은 188페이지에 있습니다.

Vocabulary in Charlotte's Web

원서에 등장하는 어려운 어휘가 정리되어 있습니다.

단어는 각 챕터별로, 원서에서 단어가 등장하는 순서 그대로 정리되어 있으며, [빈도-스펠링-발음기호-한글 뜻-영어 뜻] 순으로 표기되어 있습니다.

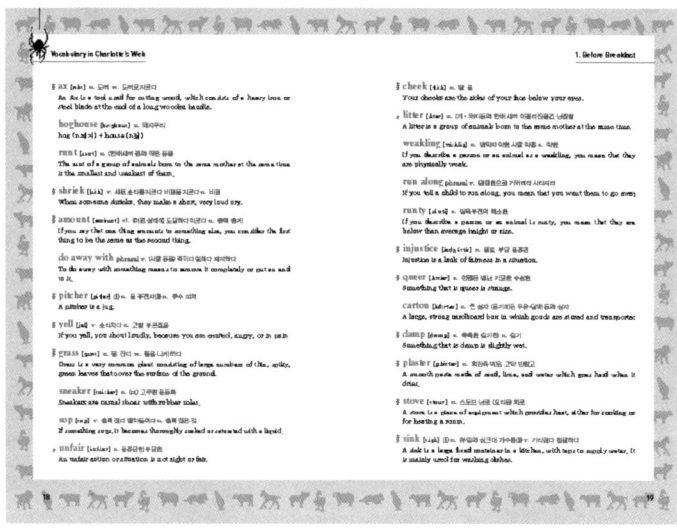

별표(★)가 많을수록 필수 어휘입니다. 또 이전 챕터에서 등장한 중요 어휘가 반복해서 나올 때는 '**복습**'이라고 표시해서 정리했습니다.

어휘 목록 중에 아주 기초적인 어휘는 제외되어 있습니다. 원서를 읽을 때 여기 나와 있는 단어 외에도 모르는 어휘가 너무 많다면, '내 영어 수준보다 지나치게 어려운 책을 골랐다'는 의미가 됩니다. 이런 경우에는 일단 더 쉬운 원서에 도전하는 것이 좋은 방법입니다.

이 책의 활용법

『원서 읽는 단어장』 이렇게 활용하세요!

모르는 단어를 일일이 손으로 쓰면서 외우려고 하지 마세요! 그런 방식으로 단어를 외웠다가는 원서 읽기를 시작하기도 전에 지쳐 쓰러져 버릴 것입니다. 아래와 같은 방식으로 문맥 속에서 자연스럽게 암기되도록 하는 것이 가장 좋습니다.

① 단어 훑어보기
원서를 읽기 전에 오늘 읽을 챕터의 단어들을 살펴봅니다. '암기'하는 것이 아니라 '단어에 익숙해진다'라는 생각으로, 스펠링과 뜻을 빠른 속도로 가볍게 살펴보는 것입니다. 특히 별표 개수가 많은 단어와 '복습'이라고 표시된 단어들을 유의 깊게 살펴보세요. 단어를 훑어보는 것만으로도 원서를 읽을 때 모르는 단어에서 오는 부담감이 많이 줄어듭니다.

② 원서 리딩
단어를 훑어봤으면, 바로 원서 리딩을 시작합니다. 훑어봤던 단어들이 눈에 띄는 것도 있고, 여전히 전혀 의미를 알 수 없는 단어들도 있을 것입니다. 하지만 모르는 단어들에 지나치게 집중하지는 마세요. 모르는 단어가 나온다고 바로 사전을 찾거나 단어장을 들추는 것은 좋지 않은 리딩 습관을 만듭니다.

리딩을 멈추고 단어를 찾는 것은, 그 단어 의미를 모르면 이야기 진행이 되지 않을 정말 중요한 단어 정도로만 한정시키세요. 나머지 모르는 단어는 문맥에 맞게 의미를 추론하고 내용에 집중하며 쭉쭉 읽어나가도록 하세요.

③ 읽은 내용 다시보기
원서를 읽고 나서, 해당 챕터의 Quiz를 풀어보고, 단어 리스트를 다시 한 번 훑어봅니다. 단, 다시보기를 할 때도 역시 단어를 쓰면서 암기하는 것이 아니라 스펠링과 의미를 빠르게 살펴보도록 합니다.

다시보기를 하다보면 처음 훑어보기를 할 때보다 익숙한 단어들이 많아졌다는 것을 알게 될 것입니다. 단어장 여백에 추가하고 싶은 단어들이나, 좋았던 문장들을 함께 적어두는 것도 매우 좋습니다.

언어학자들에 따르면, 어휘 암기는 문맥 속에서 암기했을 때 가장 회상률이 높으며, 평균적으로 15회 이상 문맥 속에서 마주칠 때 완벽히 암기하게 된다고 합니다. 위에서 말한 방식대로 영어원서와 단어장을 이용해 단어들이 문맥 속에서 자연스럽게 암기되도록 하세요! 재미있게 원서를 읽으면서 부담 없이 어휘력을 향상시킬 수 있습니다.

🐗 전문가가 알려주는 원서 읽기 Tip

Charlotte's Web의 분량과 난이도

Charlotte's Web은 총 3만 1,938단어로 이루어져 있어 중편소설 분량에 해당합니다. 영어 수준은 영어에 그리 유창하지 않은 사람이라도 한번 도전해 볼 수 있을 만큼 무난한 편입니다. 이런 이유로 남녀노소를 가리지 않고 많은 독자들이 읽고 있으며, 몇몇 특수 목적 고등학교에서는 입학시험 지문으로 사용하거나 신입생 필독서로 지정하기도 했을 정도로 널리 읽혀지고 있습니다.

오디오북을 적극적으로 활용하자

원서 읽기와 오디오북 듣기를 병행하면 리스닝 실력 향상에 큰 도움이 됩니다. 책을 읽고 나서 자투리 시간에 오디오북 듣기를 해도 좋고, 아니면 오디오북을 들으면서 눈으로 책을 읽는 것도 좋습니다. 자신의 스타일에 맞게 오디오북을 적극적으로 활용해보세요. 오디오 북은 원서와 마찬가지로 시중 서점과 인터넷 서점에서 구할 수 있습니다.

E. B. White의 책을 시리즈로 읽어보자

저자가 쓴 다양한 책을 시리즈로 읽는 것은 매우 좋은 리딩 방법입니다. 같은 저자의 작품은 유사한 어휘와 표현, 문체가 반복되므로 책을 계속 읽어나가면서 자연스러운 복습 효과를 얻을 수 있고, 이는 영어 실력 향상에 더 큰 도움을 줍니다.

특히 E. B. White는 〈Stuart Little〉, 〈The Trumpet of the Swan〉과 같은 소설들을 남겼고, 위 두 권의 소설도 〈Charlotte's Web〉과 함께 독자들에게 큰 사랑을 받고 있습니다. 〈Charlotte's Web〉을 재미있게 읽었다면 위의 책들도 꾸준히 읽어보시길 권해드립니다.

 **Let's walk in the Book**

1. Why did Mr. Arable want to go out to the hoghouse?

A. He wanted to feed the new baby pigs.

B. He wanted to kill the runt pig.

C. He wanted to show Fern the new baby pigs.

D. He heard the hogs making noises and wanted to check on them.

2. According to Mr. Arable, runt pigs _____

A. are too noisy.

B. are stronger than other pigs.

C. cannot be controlled.

D. are weak and make trouble.

3. Why did Fern think that killing the runt pig was unfair?

A. She said that the pig couldn't help being born small.

B. She said that the pig was too cute to kill.

C. She said her father was being selfish.

D. She said that the pig could get stronger when it got older.

1. Before Breakfast

4. What color was the runt pig?

A. It was white.
B. It was brown.
C. It was white and brown.
D. It was pink

5. How big was the runt pig?

A. It was bigger than a new born kitten.
B. It was no bigger than a baby goat.
C. It was no bigger than a white rat.
D. It was bigger than a dog.

Vocabulary in Charlotte's Web

ax [æks] n. 도끼; vt. 도끼로 자르다
An Ax is a tool used for cutting wood, which consists of a heavy iron or steel blade at the end of a long wooden handle.

hoghouse [hɔ́:ghaus] n. 돼지우리
hog (n. 돼지) + house (n. 집)

runt [rʌnt] n. (한배 새끼 중의) 작은 동물
The runt of a group of animals born to the same mother at the same time is the smallest and weakest of them.

shriek [ʃri:k] v. 새된 소리를 지르다, 비명을 지르다; n. 비명
When someone shrieks, they make a short, very loud cry.

amount [əmáunt] vi. (어떤 상태에) 도달하다, 이르다; n. 총액, 총계
If you say that one thing amounts to something else, you consider the first thing to be the same as the second thing.

do away with phrasal v. (사람 등을) 죽이다; 없애다, 폐지하다
To do away with something means to remove it completely or put an end to it.

pitcher [pítʃər] ① n. 물 주전자 ② n. 투수, 피처
A pitcher is a jug.

yell [jel] v. 소리치다; n. 고함, 부르짖음
If you yell, you shout loudly, because you are excited, angry, or in pain.

grass [græs] n. 풀; 잔디; vt. 풀을 나게 하다
Grass is a very common plant consisting of large numbers of thin, spiky, green leaves that cover the surface of the ground.

sneaker [sní:kər] n. (pl.) 고무창 운동화
Sneakers are casual shoes with rubber soles.

sop [sɑp] v. 흠뻑 젖다; 빨아들이다; n. 흠뻑 젖은 것
If something sops, it becomes thoroughly soaked or saturated with a liquid.

unfair [ʌ̀nfɛ́ər] a. 불공평한, 부당한
An unfair action or situation is not right or fair.

1. Before Breakfast

cheek [tʃiːk] n. 뺨, 볼
Your cheeks are the sides of your face below your eyes.

litter [lítər] n. (개·돼지 등의) 한배 새끼; 어질러진 물건, 난잡함
A litter is a group of animals born to the same mother at the same time.

weakling [wíːkliŋ] n. 병약자, 약한 사람, 약골; a. 약한
If you describe a person or an animal as a weakling, you mean that they are physically weak.

run along phrasal v. (명령형으로) 가버려라, 사라져라
If you tell a child to run along, you mean that you want them to go away.

runty [rʌ́nti] a. 발육 부전의, 왜소한
If you describe a person or an animal is runty, you mean that they are below than average height or size.

injustice [indʒʌ́stis] n. 불법, 부당, 불공평
Injustice is a lack of fairness in a situation.

queer [kwiər] a. 언짢은; 별난, 기묘한; 수상한
Something that is queer is strange.

carton [káːrtən] n. 큰 상자, (용기에 든 우유·담배 등의) 상자
A large, strong cardboard box in which goods are stored and transported.

damp [dæmp] a. 축축한, 습기 찬; n. 습기
Something that is damp is slightly wet.

plaster [plǽstər] n. 회반죽, 벽토; 고약; 반창고
A smooth paste made of sand, lime, and water which goes hard when it dries.

stove [stouv] n. 스토브, 난로; (요리용) 화로
A stove is a piece of equipment which provides heat, either for cooking or for heating a room.

sink [siŋk] ① n. (부엌의) 싱크대, 개수통 ② v. 가라앉다, 침몰하다
A sink is a large fixed container in a kitchen, with taps to supply water. It is mainly used for washing dishes.

Vocabulary in Charlotte's Web

approach [əpróutʃ] v. …에 다가가다, 가까이 가다; 다가오다; n. 접근
When you approach something, you get closer to it.

wobble [wάbəl] v. 흔들흔들하다, 떨리다; 동요하다
If something or someone wobbles, they make small movements from side to side, for example because they are unsteady.

scratch [skrætʃ] v. 할퀴다, 긁다; 갈겨쓰다; n. 긁기, 할퀴기
(scratching a. 긁히는 소리가 나는)
If a sharp object scratches someone or something, it makes small shallow cuts on their skin or surface.

lift [lift] v. 올리다, 들어 올리다; n. 올림; 차에 태워줌; 승강기
If you lift something, you move it to another position, especially upwards.

lid [lid] n. 뚜껑
A cover on a container, which can be removed.

shine [ʃain] v. (shone-shone) 빛나다, 반짝이다; 비추다; n. 빛; 광택
To produce or reflect light; To be bright.

whisper [hwíspər] v. 속삭이다, 작은 목소리로 말하다; n. 속삭임
When you whisper, you say something very quietly, using your breath rather than your throat.

rifle [ráifəl] n. 라이플 총; vt. 소총으로 쏘다; 굉장한 속도로 날리다
A rifle is a gun with a long barrel.

dagger [dǽgər] n. 단도, 단검
A dagger is a weapon like a knife with two sharp edges.

miserable [mízərəbəl] a. 불쌍한, 비참한, 딱한, 가엾은
Something that is miserable is very unhappy or uncomfortable.

specimen [spésəmən] n. 견본, 표본, 실례, 예
A specimen of something is an example of it which gives an idea of what the whole of it is like.

1. Before Breakfast

pop [pɑp] n. (구어) 아버지, 아빠; 아저씨
Some people call their father pop.

be along idiom (미래시제로) 당도하다, 오다; 따라붙다

✲ **distribute** [distríbju:t] v. 분배하다, 배분하다; 골고루 퍼뜨리다
If you distribute things, you hand them or deliver them to a number of people.

✲ **daylight** [déilàit] n. 낮; 일광; 빛
Daylight is the time of day when it begins to get light.

✲ **rid** [rid] v. 없애다, 제거하다
When you get rid of something, you take action so that you no longer have it or suffer from it.

✲ **prompt** [prɑmpt] a. 신속한, 재빠른; 즉석의; vt. 자극하다 (promptly ad. 신속히, 즉시)
A prompt action is done without any delay.

nursing bottle [nə́:rsiŋ bɑ́tl] n. 젖병
A nursing bottle is a plastic bottle with a special rubber top through which a baby can suck milk or another liquid.

✲ **rubber** [rʌ́bər] n. 고무
Rubber is a strong, waterproof, elastic substance made from the juice of a tropical tree or produced chemically.

nipple [nípəl] n. (젖병의) 고무 젖꼭지; 젖꼭지
A nipple is a piece of rubber or plastic which is fitted to the top of a baby's bottle.

✲ **infant** [ínfənt] n. 유아, 갓난아기; a. 유아(용)의; 유치한, 초기의
An infant is a baby or very young child.

✲ **suck** [sʌk] v. 빨다, 빨아들이다, 흡수하다; n. 빨기
If you suck something, you hold it in your mouth and pull at it with the muscles in your cheeks and tongue.

✲ **tiny** [táini] a. 직은, 조그마한
Something or someone that is tiny is extremely small.

Vocabulary in Charlotte's Web

appetite [ǽpitàit] n. 식욕, 욕구
Your appetite is your desire to eat.

catch on phrasal v. 이해하다, 터득하다
If you catch on to something, you understand it, or realize that it is happening.

honk [hɔ:ŋk] v. 경적을 울리다, 울다; n. 경적 소리
If you honk the horn of a vehicle or if the horn honks, you make the horn produce a short loud sound.

slip [slip] v. 미끄러지다, 미끄러지게 하다; n. 미끄럼, 실수
If you slip somewhere, you go there quickly and quietly.

grab [græb] v. 부여잡다, 움켜쥐다; n. 부여잡기
If you grab something, you take it or pick it up suddenly and roughly.

notice [nóutis] n. 주의, 주목; vt. 알아차리다, 주의하다
If you take no notice of someone or something, you do not consider them to be important enough to affect what you think or what you do.

blissful [blísfəl] a. 더없이 행복한; 즐거운
A blissful situation or period of time is one in which you are extremely happy.

charge [tʃɑ:rdʒ] n. 책임, 의무; 청구 금액; v. 부담시키다, 청구하다
If you take charge of someone or something, you make yourself responsible for them and take control over them.

capital [kǽpitl] n. 수도; 중심지; 자본; 대문자; a. 자본의; 가장 중요한; 대문자의
The capital of a country is the city or town where its government or parliament meets.

dreamy [drí:mi] a. 꿈꾸는 듯한; 꿈 많은 (dreamily ad. 꿈꾸듯이)
Looking as though you are thinking about other things and not paying attention to what is happening around you.

pupil [pjú:pəl] ① n. 학생, 제자 ② n. 눈동자, 동공
The pupils of a school are the children who go to it.

1. Before Breakfast

* **giggle** [gígəl] v. 낄낄 웃다; n. 낄낄 웃음
  If someone giggles, they laugh in a childlike way, because they are amused, nervous, or embarrassed.

* **blush** [blʌʃ] v. 얼굴을 붉히다, (얼굴이) 빨개지다; n. 얼굴을 붉힘, 홍조
  When you blush, your face becomes redder than usual because you are ashamed or embarrassed.

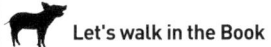 Let's walk in the Book

1. **Which of the following did Fern NOT do with Wilbur?**
   A. She fed him.
   B. She warmed up his milk in the morning.
   C. She let Wilbur sleep in her bed.
   D. She held his bottle for him.

2. **Where did Wilbur live when he turned two weeks old?**
   A. He lived next to the kitchen.
   B. He lived in the woodshed.
   C. He lived outside.
   D. He lived in Fern's room.

2. Willbur

3. How did Wilbur stay warm at night?

   A. He slept under straw.

   B. He used a blanket Fern made for him.

   C. He covered himself with mud.

   D. He slept in a pile of leaves.

4. Which of the following is NOT true?

   A. Fern took Wilbur upstairs with her.

   B. Fern took Wilbur on walks with her dolls.

   C. Fern took Wilbur into the house.

   D. Wilbur followed Fern around after school.

5. Why didn't Wilbur go swimming with Fern and the other children?

   A. The other children didn't want to swim with Wilbur.

   B. Fern didn't let Wilbur in the water.

   C. Wilbur thought the water was too cold.

   D. Wilbur liked playing in the grass instead.

Vocabulary in Charlotte's Web

stroke [strouk] ① vt. 쓰다듬다, 어루만지다; n. 쓰다듬기, 달램 ② n. 타격, 일격; 발작
If you stroke someone or something, you move your hand slowly and gently over them.

feed [fi:d] v. (fed-fed) (동물 등에) 먹이를 주다; 양육하다; n. 먹이, 사료
If you feed a person or animal, you give them food to eat and sometimes actually put it in their mouths.

bib [bib] n. 턱받이; (앞치마 등의) 가슴 부분
A bib is a piece of cloth or plastic which is worn by very young children to protect their clothes while they are eating.

suppertime [sʌ́pərtàim] n. 저녁 식사 시간 (보통 오후 5-7시 사이)
Suppertime is the period of the day when people have their supper. It can be in the early part of the evening or just before they go to bed at night.

gaze [geiz] vi. 뚫어지게 보다, 응시하다; n. 응시, 주시
If you gaze at someone or something, you look steadily at them for a long time.

adore [ədɔ́:r] vt. 숭배[동경]하다; 아주 좋아하다 (adoring a. 매우 좋아하는; 숭배하는)
If you adore something, you like it very much.

woodshed [wúdʃèd] n. 목재 헛간 (wood 나무, 목재 + shed 오두막, 우리)
A woodshed is a small building which is used for storing wood for a fire.

blossom [blásəm] n. 꽃; vi. 꽃 피다
Blossom is the flowers that appear on a tree before the fruit.

yard [jɑ:rd] n. 마당, 뜰; (가축의) 우리, 축사
A yard is a piece of land next to someone's house, with grass and plants growing in it.

straw [strɔ:] n. 짚, 밀짚; 스트로, 빨대
Straw consists of the dried, yellowish stalks from crops such as wheat or barley.

doorway [dɔ́:rwèi] n. 문간, 현관, 출입구
A doorway is a space in a wall where a door opens and closes.

2. Willbur

* **grunt** [grʌnt] vi. (돼지가) 꿀꿀거리다; (사람이) 툴툴거리다; n. 꿀꿀[툴툴]거리는 소리
  When an animal grunts, it makes a low rough noise.

* **peer** [piər] vi. 자세히 보다, 응시하다; 희미하게 나타나다
  If you peer at something, you look at it very hard.

* **poke** [pouk] v. 찌르다, 쑤시다, 들이대다; n. 찌름, 쑤심
  If you poke someone or something, you quickly push them with your finger or with a sharp object.

  snout [snaut] n. (돼지 등의) 코, 주둥이
  The snout of an animal such as a pig is its long nose.

** **dig** [dig] v. (dug-dug) 파다, 파헤치다; 찌르다; 탐구하다; n. 파기
  If you dig one thing into another or if one thing digs into another, the first thing is pushed hard into the second, or presses hard into it.

* **crawl** [krɔːl] vi. 기어가다, 느릿느릿 가다; n. 기어감; 서행
  When you crawl, you move forward on your hands and knees.

* **enchant** [entʃǽnt] vt. 매혹하다, 황홀케 하다
  If you are enchanted by someone or something, they cause you to have feelings of great delight or pleasure.

* **vanish** [vǽniʃ] v. 사라지다, 없어지다, 모습을 감추다
  If someone or something vanishes, they disappear suddenly or in a way that cannot be explained.

* **carriage** [kǽridʒ] n. 유모차; 탈것, 차
  A baby carriage is a small vehicle in which a baby can lie as it is pushed along.

** **journey** [dʒə́ːrni] n. 여행
  When you make a journey, you travel from one place to another.

* **alongside** [əlɔ́ːŋsàid] ad., prep. (…에) 옆으로 대고
  If one thing is alongside another thing, the first thing is next to the second.

* **blanket** [blǽŋkit] n. 담요; 덮개
  A blanket is a large square or rectangular piece of thick cloth, especially one which you put on a bed to keep you warm.

Vocabulary in Charlotte's Web

* **lash** [læʃ] ① n. (= eyelash) 속눈썹 ② v. 세차게 부딪히다; 심하게 움직이다
  Your lashes are the hairs that grow on the edge of your upper and lower eyelids.

  bathing suit [béiðiŋ su:t] n. (= swimsuit) 수영복
  A bathing suit is a piece of clothing which people wear when they go swimming.

* **brook** [bruk] ① n. 시내, 개천 ② vt. 견디다, 참다
  A brook is a small stream.

  tag along phrasal v. 따르다
  If someone goes somewhere and you tag along, you go with them, especially when they have not asked you to.

* **heel** [hi:l] n. (발) 뒤꿈치; (동물의) 발; 뒤축
  Your heel is the back part of your foot, just below your ankle.

* **wade** [weid] vi. (개천 등을) 걸어서 건너다; (물·눈·인파 등의 속을) 고생하며 나아가다
  If you wade through something that makes it difficult to walk, usually water or mud, you walk through it.

* **splash** [splæʃ] v. (물·흙탕물 등을) 튀기다; n. 물 튀기기, 첨벙 (물 튀기는 소리)
  If you splash water, you hit or disturb the water in a noisy way, causing some of it to fly up into the air.

* **amuse** [əmjú:z] vt. 즐겁게 하다, 재미나게 하다
  If something amuses you, it makes you want to laugh or smile.

* **edge** [edʒ] n. 가장자리, 끝; 변두리
  The edge of something is the place or line where it stops, or the part of it that is furthest from the middle.

* **moist** [mɔist] a. 축축한, 습한, 습기 있는
  Something that is moist is slightly wet.

* **sticky** [stíki] a. 끈적(끈끈)한, 들러붙는
  A sticky substance is soft, or thick and liquid, and can stick to other things.

2. Willbur

* **ooze** [uːz] ① v. 스며 나오다, 새어나오다 ② n. 보드라운 진흙, 습지
  (oozy a. 스며 나오는, 새는)
  If a thick liquid oozes from a place, or if something oozes a thick liquid, the liquid flows from the place slowly.

* **weep** [wiːp] v. 눈물을 흘리다, 울다
  If someone weeps, they cry.

* **firm** [fəːrm] a. 굳은, 단단한, 견고한; n. 회사
  If something is firm, it does not change much in shape when it is pressed but is not completely hard.

* **scrap** [skræp] n. 찌꺼기, 부스러기; 작은 조각, 파편
  Scraps are pieces of unwanted food which are thrown away or given to animals.

* **arrange** [əréindʒ] v. (미리) 정하다, 준비하다; 가지런히 하다, 배열하다
  If you arrange with someone to do something, you make plans with them to do it.

  holler [hálər] v. 고함지르다, 외치다; n. 외침, 고함
  If you holler, you shout loudly.

* **barn** [bɑːrn] n. (농가의) 헛간, 광
  A barn is a building on a farm in which crops or animal food can be kept.

* **manure** [mənjúər] n. 비료, 거름, 퇴비; vt. (땅에) 비료를[거름을] 주다
  Manure is animal faeces, sometimes mixed with chemicals, that is spread on the ground in order to make plants grow healthy and strong.

* **pile** [pail] n. 쌓아 올린 더미; 다수, 대량; v. 쌓아 올리다; 쌓이다
  A pile of things is a mass of them that is high in the middle and has sloping sides.

* **cellar** [sélər] n. 지하실, 지하층
  A cellar is a room underneath a building, which is often used for storing things in.

Let's walk in the Book

1. **What was Fern allowed to do in the barn with Wilbur?**
   A. She was allowed to play with Wilbur.
   B. She was allowed to watch Wilbur.
   C. She was allowed to take Wilbur out for walks.
   D. She was allowed to go inside the pigpen with Wilbur.

2. **What didn't Wilbur do when he was bored in the pigpen?**
   A. He checked his food trough.
   B. He scratched his back on the fence.
   C. He sat on top of the manure pile.
   D. He played with the goose in the pigpen.

3. Escape

3. Who suggested that Wilbur leave his pigpen?

    A. A goose

    B. A cocker spaniel

    C. A duck

    D. A cow

4. How was Wilbur able to leave his pigpen?

    A. There was a loose board on the fence.

    B. The goose opened the gate for him.

    C. Wilbur pushed the gate door open.

    D. Wilbur dug a hole under the fence.

5. Who first saw Wilbur out of his pen?

    A. Mr. Zuckerman

    B. Mrs. Zuckerman

    C. Lurvy

    D. The cocker spaniel

Vocabulary in Charlotte's Web

* **hay** [hei] n. 건초, 말린 풀
  Hay is grass which has been cut and dried so that it can be used to feed animals.

* **perspire** [pərspáiər] v. 땀을 흘리다, 발한하다, 발산시키다 (perspiration n. 땀, 발한 작용)
  When you perspire, a liquid comes out on the surface of your skin, because you are hot or frightened.

* **patient** [péiʃənt] ① a. 인내심[참을성] 있는, 끈기 있는 ② n. 환자, 병자
  If you are patient, you stay calm and do not get annoyed.

* **grain** [grein] n. 곡물, 낟알; 미량
  Grain is a cereal crop, especially wheat or corn, that has been harvested and is used for food or in trade.

* **harness** [háːrnis] n. 마구; 장치, 장비, 작업 설비; vt. 마구를 채우다
  A harness is a set of leather straps and metal links fastened round a horse's head or body so that the horse can have a carriage, cart, or plough fastened to it.

* **axle** [ǽksəl] n. 굴대, 축
  An axle is a rod connecting a pair of wheels on a car or other vehicle.

* **grease** [griːs] n. (윤활유 등의) 기름; 그리스; vt. …에 기름을 바르대[치다]
  Grease is a thick, oily substance which is put on the moving parts of cars and other machines in order to make them work smoothly.

* **loft** [lɔːft] n. (짚·건초 등을 저장하는) 다락; 지붕밑 방
  A loft is the space inside the sloping roof of a house or other building, where things are sometimes stored.

* **pitch** [pitʃ] v. 던지다, 처박다; n. 던지기; 설득, 선전
  If you pitch something somewhere, you throw it with quite a lot of force.

* **breeze** [briːz] n. 산들바람, 미풍
  A breeze is a gentle wind.

* **stall** [stɔːl] n. 마구간[외양간]의 한 칸, 마구간; 진열대; vt. 마구간에 넣다; 꼼짝 못하게 하다
  A stall or stalls is a building in which horses are kept.

3. Escape

* **tie-up** [táiʌp] ① n. 소 외양간 ② n. 정체, 교통 체증; 긴박한 상황
  A tie-up is a building where cows are kept or milked.

  sheepfold [ʃíːpfòuld] n. 양우리
  sheep (n. 양) + fold (n. 우리)

  pigpen [pígpen] n. 돼지우리
  A pigpen is an enclosed place where pigs are kept on a farm.

* **ladder** [lǽdər] n. 사다리
  A ladder is a piece of equipment used for climbing up something or down from something.

* **grindstone** [gráindstòun] n. 맷돌; 회전 숫돌
  A grindstone is a large round stone that turns like a wheel and is used for sharpening knives and tools.

  pitch fork [pitʃfɔːrk] n. 건초용 포크, (세 가닥) 갈퀴
  A pitch fork is an agricultural tool with a long handle and long, thin, widely separated pointed tines used to lift and pitch.

  monkey wrench [mʌ́ŋki rentʃ] n. 멍커렌치 (목에 나사를 장치해 아가리를 자유로이 조절할 수 있는 공업 용구)
  A monkey wrench is an adjustable metal tool used for tightening or loosening metal nuts of different sizes.

* **scythe** [saið] n. (자루가 긴) 풀·곡물 베는 낫
  A scythe is a tool with a long curved blade at right angles to a long handle.

* **lawn** [lɔːn] n. 잔디, 잔디밭
  A lawn is an area of grass that is kept cut short and is usually part of someone's garden or backyard, or part of a park.

* **mower** [móuər] n. 잔디 깎는 기계, 풀[보리] 베는 기계
  A mower is a machine for cutting grass on lawns.

* **pail** [peil] n. 들통, 버킷
  A pail is a bucket, usually made of metal or wood.

Vocabulary in Charlotte's Web

* **bucket** [bʌ́kit] n. 버킷, 물통; 양동이
  A bucket is a round metal or plastic container with a handle attached to its sides.

* **sack** [sæk] n. 부대, 마대, 자루; vt. 부대[자루]에 넣다; 해고[파면]하다
  A sack is a large bag made of rough woven material.

* **rust** [rʌst] n. (금속의) 녹; v. 녹슬다, 부식하다 (rusty a. 녹슨)
  Rust is a brown substance that forms on iron or steel, when it comes into contact with water.

* **swallow** [swálou] ① n. 제비 ② vt. 들이켜다, 삼키다, 꿀꺽 삼키다
  A swallow is a kind of small bird with pointed wings and a forked tail.

** **nest** [nest] n. 둥지, 보금자리
  A bird's nest is the home that it makes to lay its eggs in.

** **stool** [stu:l] n. (등이 없는) 걸상; 발판(대)
  A stool is a seat with legs but no support for your arms or back.

* **discard** [diská:rd] vt. 버리다, 처분하다; n. 버림(받음)
  If you discard something, you get rid of it because you no longer want it or need it.

** **trust** [trʌst] v. 신뢰하다, 믿다; n. 신뢰, 신용, 신임
  If you trust someone, you believe that they are honest and sincere and will not deliberately do anything to harm you.

* **goose** [gu:s] n. (pl. geese) 거위; 거위 고기
  A goose is a large bird that has a long neck and webbed feet.

** **allow** [əláu] v. 허락하다, 허가하다; 주다
  If someone is allowed to do something, it is all right for them to do it and they will not get into trouble.

** **wander** [wándər] v. (정처 없이) 돌아다니다, 방랑하다
  If you wander in a place, you walk around there in a casual way, often without intending to go in any particular direction.

3. Escape

* **trough** [trɔ(:)f] n. 구유, 여물통
A trough is a long narrow container from which farm animals drink or eat.

* **sniff** [snif] v. 코를 킁킁거리다, 냄새를 맡다
When you sniff, you breathe in air through your nose hard enough to make a sound.

* **overlook** [òuvərlúk] vt. 못 보고 지나치다, 빠뜨리고 못 보다; 눈감아주다
If you overlook a fact or problem, you do not notice it, or do not realize how important it is.

* **strip** [strip] n. 가늘고 긴 조각, 한 조각; v. (껍질 등을) 벗기다, 떼어버리다
A strip of something such as paper, cloth, or food is a long, narrow piece of it.

* **itch** [itʃ] vi. 가렵다, 근질근질하다; n. 가려움; 안달
When a part of your body itches, you have an unpleasant feeling on your skin that makes you want to scratch.

* **fence** [fens] n. 울타리, 담; 장애물
A fence is a barrier between two areas of land, made of wood or wire supported by posts.

* **rub** [rʌb] v. 비비다, 문지르다; n. 문지르기, 마찰
If you rub against a surface or rub a part of your body against a surface, you move it backwards and forwards while pressing it against the surface.

* **board** [bɔːrd] n. 판자; 칠판, 게시판; v. (탈것 등에) 타다; 하숙하다
Boards are long flat pieces of wood which are used, for example, to make floors or walls.

* **risk** [risk] n. 위험(성); 모험; vt. 위태롭게 하다
If there is a risk of something unpleasant, there is a possibility that it will happen.

* **squeeze** [skwiːz] vt. 꽉 쥐다; 압착하다, 짜내다
If you squeeze something, you press it firmly, usually with your hands.

* **chuckle** [tʃʌ́kl] vi. 낄낄 웃다; n. 낄낄 웃음
When you chuckle, you laugh quietly.

Vocabulary in Charlotte's Web

- **queer** [kwiər] a. 언짢은; 별난, 기묘한; 수상한
  Something that is queer is strange.

- **orchard** [ɔ́ːrtʃərd] n. 과수원
  An orchard is an area of land on which fruit trees are grown.

- **root** [ruːt] ① v. (돼지 등이) 코로 땅을 파서 먹을 것을 찾다 ② n. 뿌리, 근원; v. 뿌리박다, 정착하다
  If you root through or in something, you search for something by moving other things around.

- **sod** [sɑd] n. 잔디, 잔디밭
  The sod is the surface of the earth, with the grass and roots that are growing in it.

- **radish** [rǽdiʃ] n. [식물] 무
  Radishes are small red or white vegetables that are the roots of a plant.

- **oat** [out] n. 귀리 (오트밀의 원료, 가축의 사료)
  The oat is a species of cereal grain grown for its seed.

- **prance** [præns] vi. 껑충거리며 나아가다, 여기저기 뛰어 다니다
  When a horse prances, it moves with quick, high steps.

- **stroll** [stróul] vi. 한가롭게 거닐다, 산책하다
  If you stroll somewhere, you walk there in a slow, relaxed way.

- **twirl** [twəːrl] v. 빙빙 돌다, 회전하다; (손가락으로) 빼배 꼬다; n. 회전, 선회
  If you twirl something or if it twirls, it turns around and around with a smooth, fairly fast movement.

- **pause** [pɔːz] v. 중단하다, 잠시 멈추다; n. 잠깐 멈춤, 중지
  If you pause while you are doing something, you stop for a short period and then continue.

- **shade** [ʃeid] n. 그늘, 응달; vt. 그늘지게 하다, 어둡게 하다
  Shade is an area of darkness under or next to an object such as a tree, where sunlight does not reach.

3. Escape

plow [plau] v. (밭을) 갈다, 경작하다; n. 쟁기
When someone plows an area of land, they turn over the soil.

immediate [imí:diət] a. 즉각의, 당장의 (immediately ad. 곧, 즉각, 즉시)
An immediate result, action, or reaction happens or is done without any delay.

racket [rǽkit] ① n. 떠드는 소리, 소음; 법석 ② n. 라켓
A racket is a loud unpleasant noise.

cocker spaniel [kákərspǽnjəl] n. 코커스패니얼 (사냥·애완용 개)
A cocker spaniel is a breed of small dog with silky hair and long ears.

commotion [kəmóuʃən] n. 동요, 소동, 소요
A commotion is a lot of noise, confusion, and excitement.

chase [tʃeis] n. 추격, 사냥; v. 뒤쫓다, 추적[추격]하다
The chase is the activity of hunting animals.

shed [ʃed] n. 광, (간이) 창고; 오두막
A shed is a small building that is used for storing things such as garden tools.

mend [mend] v. 수선하다, 고치다; n. 수선, 개량
If you mend something that is broken or not working, you repair it, so that it works properly or can be used.

hire [háiər] v. 고용하다, 빌리다; n. 고용; 임차
If you hire someone, you employ them or pay them to do a particular job for you.

asparagus [əspǽrəgəs] n. 아스파라거스
Asparagus is a vegetable that is long and green and has small shoots at one end.

patch [pætʃ] n. (채소나 과일을 기르는) 작은 땅; 헝겊 조각; v. 헝겊을 대고 깁다; 수선하다
A patch of land is a small area of land where a particular plant or crop grows.

Vocabulary in Charlotte's Web

⁑ weed [wi:d] n. 잡초; v. 잡초를 없애다, 김매다
A weed is a wild plant that grows in gardens or fields of crops and prevents the plants that you want from growing properly.

⁑ rush [rʌʃ] v. 돌진하다, 서두르다; 돌진시키다, 서두르게 하다
If you rush somewhere, you go there quickly.

slop [slɑp] n. (돼지 사료용) 밥찌꺼기; 엎지름, 흙탕물; v. 엎지르다, 엎질러서 더럽히다
You can use slop or slops to refer to liquid waste containing the remains of food.

⁑ lamb [læm] n. 새끼 양
A lamb is a young sheep.

prick up phrasal v. 귀를 쫑긋 세우다
If someone pricks up their ears or if their ears prick up, they listen eagerly when they suddenly hear an interesting sound or an important piece of information.

⁑ stir [stəːr] v. 움직이다; 휘젓다; n. 휘젓기, 뒤섞음
If you stir, you move slightly, for example because you are uncomfortable or beginning to wake up.

⁑ pen [pen] ① vt. 우리[축사] 안에 넣다; n. 우리, 축사 ② n. 펜촉, 펜
If people or animals are penned somewhere or are penned up, they are forced to remain in a very small area.

⁎ sneak [sni:k] v. 살금살금 움직이다, 숨기다 (sneak up phrasal v. 몰래 다가가다)
If you sneak somewhere, you go there very quietly on foot, trying to avoid being seen or heard.

⁑ awful [ɔ́ːfəl] a. 지독한, 대단한; 무서운
If you say that something is awful, you mean that it is extremely unpleasant, shocking, or bad.

⁎ dodge [dɑdʒ] v. 홱 피하다, 날쌔게 비키다
If you dodge, you move suddenly, often to avoid being hit, caught, or seen.

3. Escape

- **skip** [skip] v. 뛰어다니다, 깡충깡충 뛰다; 건너뛰다, 빠뜨리다
  If you skip along, you move almost as if you are dancing, with a series of little jumps from one foot to the other.

- **spring** [spriŋ] vi. (sprang–sprung) 뛰다, 솟아오르다; n. 봄, 튀어 오름, 용수철
  When a person or animal springs, they jump upwards or forwards suddenly or quickly.

- **hind** [haind] a. 뒤쪽의, 후방의
  An animal's hind legs are at the back of its body.

- **grab** [græb] v. 부여잡다, 움켜쥐다; n. 부여잡기
  If you grab something, you take it or pick it up suddenly and roughly.

- **cheer** [tʃiər] v. 갈채하다, 응원하다; 기운을 북돋우다; n. 환호, 갈채
  When people cheer, they shout loudly to show their approval or to encourage someone.

- **downhill** [dáunhìl] n. 내리막길; 몰락
  If something or someone is moving downhill or is downhill, they are moving down a slope or are located towards the bottom of a hill.

- **gander** [gǽndər] n. 거위의 수컷
  A gander is a male goose.

- **uphill** [ʌ́phìl] n. 오르막길; 치받이
  If something or someone is uphill or is moving uphill, they are near the top of a hill or are going up a slope.

- **honk** [hɔːŋk] v. (기러기가) 울다; 경적을 울리다
  when a goose honks, it makes a loud noise.

- **rooster** [rúːstər] n. 수탉
  A rooster is an adult male chicken.

- **daze** [deiz] vt. 멍하게 하다; 눈부시게 하다; 현혹시키다
  If someone is dazed, they are confused and unable to think clearly, often because of shock or a blow to the head.

Vocabulary in Charlotte's Web

hullabaloo [hʌ́ləbəlùː] n. 와글와글[왁자지껄] 하는 소리, 소란
A hullabaloo is a lot of noise or fuss made by people who are angry or excited about something.

⁎ fuss [fʌs] n. 야단법석, 호들갑; 몸달아 설침, 흥분
Fuss is anxious or excited behavior which serves no useful purpose.

⁎ barely [béərli] ad. 간신히, 겨우, 가까스로
You use barely to say that something is only just true or only just the case.

⁑ comfort [kʌ́mfərt] vt. 위로하다, 안락하게 하다; n. 위안, 안락
If you comfort someone, you make them feel less worried, unhappy, or upset, for example by saying kind things to them.

⁑ wheat [hwiːt] n. 밀, 소맥
Wheat is a cereal crop grown for food.

middling [mídliŋ] n. (밀기울 섞인) 거친 밀가루; a. 중간치의, 중등의
A middlings purifier is a device used in the production of flour to remove the husks from the kernels of wheat.

popover [pápòuvər] n. 살짝 구운 과자의 일종
A popover is a light, hollow roll made from an egg batter.

⁎ tap [tæp] ① v. 가볍게 두드리다; n. 가볍게 두드리기 ② n. 주둥이, (수도 등의) 꼭지
If you tap something, you hit it with a quick light blow or a series of quick light blows.

⁎ lure [luər] vt. 유혹하다, 불러들이다; n. 유혹하는 것
To lure someone means to trick them into a particular place or to trick them into doing something that they should not do.

captivity [kæptívəti] n. 포로
Captivity is the state of being kept imprisoned or enclosed.

⁑ appeal [əpíːl] vi. 마음에 호소하다; 애원하다, 간청하다; n. 애원, 간청
If you appeal to someone to do something, you make a serious and urgent request to them.

3. Escape

* **stomach** [stʌ́mək] n. 위; 복부, 배
  Your stomach is the organ inside your body where food is digested before it moves into the intestines.

* **innocent** [ínəsnt] a. 순진한, 천진난만한; 결백한 (innocently ad. 순진하게)
  If someone is innocent, they have no experience or knowledge of the more complex or unpleasant aspects of life.

** **worth** [wəːrθ] a. …의 가치가 있는; n. 가치, 값어치
  If something is worth a particular amount of money, it can be sold for that amount or is considered to have that value.

* **barrel** [bǽrəl] n. 통; 한 통의 분량, 1배럴
  A barrel is a large, round container for liquids or food.

* **reconsider** [rìːkənsídər] v. 재고하다, 다시 생각하다
  If you reconsider a decision or opinion, you think about it and try to decide whether it should be changed.

* **fetch** [fetʃ] vt. 가져오다, 데려오다, 불러오다
  If you fetch something or someone, you go and get them from the place where they are.

8-penny nail n. 2.5인치 길이의 못

* **praise** [preiz] n. 칭찬, 찬양; vt. 칭찬하다
  Praise is what you say or write about someone when you are praising them.

Let's walk in the Book

1. **Why was Wilbur's plan ruined?**
   A. It was raining.
   B. It was too cold for Wilbur to go for a walk.
   C. Nobody would play with Wilbur.
   D. Wilbur felt sick.

2. **Who was Templeton?**
   A. Templeton was a mouse.
   B. Templeton was a goose.
   C. Templeton was a lamb.
   D. Templeton was a rat.

4. Loneliness

3. Why couldn't Fern visit Wilbur?

   A. She had school all day.

   B. She was busy playing with her friends.

   C. It was raining.

   D. She was only allowed to visit Wilbur on the weekends.

4. Why didn't Wilbur eat his breakfast?

   A. Wilbur didn't like the food that Lurvy gave him.

   B. Wilbur wanted love rather than food.

   C. Wilbur didn't want to get wet.

   D. Wilbur felt sick and needed medicine.

5. Why wouldn't the goose play with Wilbur?

   A. The goose was too busy eating.

   B. The goose needed to sit on its eggs.

   C. The goose didn't want to get wet.

   D. The goose refused to play with pigs.

Vocabulary in Charlotte's Web

* **roof** [ru:f] n. 지붕; 최고부, 꼭대기
  The roof of a building is the covering on top of it that protects the people and things inside from the weather.

* **drip** [drip] v. 물방울이 떨어지다; n. 똑똑 떨어지기
  When liquid drips somewhere, or you drip it somewhere, it falls in individual small drops.

* **eaves** [i:vz] n. (pl.) 처마, 차양
  The eaves of a house are the lower edges of its roof.

* **crook** [kruk] vt. 구부리다, (활처럼) 굽히다; n. 굽은 것, 갈고리
  If you crook your arm or finger, you bend it.

* **lane** [lein] n. 좁은 길, 골목길
  A lane is a narrow road, especially in the country.

* **thistle** [θísl] n. [식물] 엉겅퀴 (스코틀랜드의 국화)
  A thistle is a wild plant which has leaves with sharp points and purple flowers.

* **pigweed** [pígwì:d] n. [식물] 명아주, 흰 명아주
  A pigweed is a fast-growing weed that has been noted as a threat to production of genetically modified cotton and soybean crops.

* **spatter** [spǽtər] v. 튀기다, 물장구치다, 흩뿌리다; n. 튀김, 튀기는 소리
  If a liquid spatters a surface or you spatter a liquid over a surface, drops of the liquid fall on an area of the surface.

* **gush** [gʌʃ] vi. 세차게 흘러나오다, 분출하다; n. 분출, 솟아나옴
  When liquid gushes out of something, or when something gushes a liquid, the liquid flows out very quickly and in large quantities.

* **downspout** [dáunspàut] n. 수직 낙수 홈통
  A downspout is a pipe attached to the side of a building, through which water flows from the roof into a drain.

* **graze** [greiz] v. 풀을 뜯어먹다; 방목하다; n. 방목, 목축
  When animals graze or are grazed, they eat the grass or other plants that are growing in a particular place.

4. Loneliness

* **meadow** [médou] n. 목초지, 초원
A meadow is a field which has grass and flowers growing in it.

fold [fould] ① n. 우리; vt. 우리에 넣다 ② v. 접다, 개다; n. 주름, 접은 자리
A fold is a small area of a field surrounded by a fence where sheep can be put for shelter for the night.

skim milk [skim milk] n. 탈지 우유 (지방 함량을 0.1% 이내로 줄인 우유)
Skim milk is milk that contains less fat than normal because the cream has been removed from it.

* **crust** [krʌst] n. 빵 껍질; 딱딱한 외피
The crust on a loaf of bread is the outside part.

* **maple** [méipəl] n. 단풍나무
A maple or a maple tree is a tree with five-pointed leaves which turn bright red or gold in autumn.

leftover [léftòuvər] a. 나머지의, 남은; n. 나머지, 찌꺼기
You use leftover to describe an amount of something that remains after the rest of it has been used or eaten.

* **custard** [kʌ́stərd] n. 커스터드 (우유·계란에 설탕·향료를 넣어서 찐[구운] 과자)
Custard is a sweet yellow sauce made from milk and eggs or from milk and a powder. It is eaten with fruit and puddings.

* **raisin** [réizən] n. 건포도
Raisins are dried grapes.

Shredded Wheat n. 아침 식사용의 곡물 식품
Shredded Wheat is a breakfast cereal made from whole wheat.

* **trench** [trentʃ] n. 도랑, 굴; v. 도랑을 파다, (논밭을) 파헤치다
A trench is a long narrow channel that is cut into the ground.

** **bury** [béri] vt. 묻다, 파묻다, 매장하다
To bury something means to put it into a hole in the ground and cover it up with earth.

Vocabulary in Charlotte's Web

* **dirt** [də:rt] n. 진흙; 쓰레기; 흙
If there is dirt on something, there is dust, mud, or a stain on it.

paring [pέəriŋ] n. 벗긴[깎은] 껍질, 부스러기; 껍질 벗기기, 깎기
Parings are thin pieces that have been cut off things such as a fingernails, fruit, or vegetables.

* **gravy** [gréivi] n. 육즙, 고깃국물
Gravy is a sauce made from the juices that come from meat when it cooks.

scraping [skréipiŋ] n. 깎은 부스러기, 긁어모은 것; 먼지
Scraping is a small amount of something produced by scratching a surface.

scrap [skræp] n. 찌꺼기, 부스러기; 작은 조각, 파편
Scraps are pieces of unwanted food which are thrown away or given to animals.

* **stale** [steil] a. (음식 따위가) 상한, 신선하지 않은
Stale food is no longer fresh or good to eat.

hominy [háməni] n. (미) 묽게 탄 옥수수(죽)
Hominy is dried maize which is boiled in water or milk.

* **supper** [sʌ́pər] n. 저녁 식사, (가벼운) 만찬
Supper is a simple meal eaten just before you go to bed at night.

provender [právindər] n. 여물 (주로 건초와 같아서 빻은 곡물); vt. 여물을 주다
Provender is crops that are grown as food for cattle and horses.

* **wrapper** [rǽpər] n. 싸는 것, 포장지; 싸는 사람
A wrapper is a piece of paper, plastic, or thin metal which covers and protects something that you buy, especially food.

* **prune** [pru:n] ① n. 서양 자두, 말린 자두 ② vt. (가지·뿌리 등을) 잘라내다, 치다
A prune is a dried plum.

* **morsel** [mɔ́:rsəl] n. 한 입, 소량; vt. 작은 양을 주다
A morsel is a very small amount of something, especially a very small piece of food.

4. Loneliness

* **marmalade** [mά:rməlèid] n. 마멀레이드 (오렌지·레몬 등으로 만든 잼)
  Marmalade is a food made from oranges, lemons, or grapefruit that is similar to jam.

* **bake** [beik] v. (빵·과자 등을) 굽다
  If you bake, you spend some time preparing and mixing together ingredients to make bread, cakes, pies, or other food which is cooked in the oven.

* **upsidedown** [ʌ́psaiddáun] ad. 거꾸로, 뒤집혀; 엉망으로, 뒤죽박죽으로
  If something has been moved upside down, it has been turned round so that the part that is usually lowest is above the part that is usually highest.

* **groan** [groun] v. 신음하다, 끙끙거리다; n. 신음[끙끙거리는] 소리
  If you groan, you make a long, low sound because you are in pain, or because you are upset or unhappy about something.

* **honest** [άnist] a. 정직한, 숨김없는, 거짓 없는; 진실[성실]한 (honestly ad. 솔직히, 정말로)
  If you are honest in a particular situation, you tell the complete truth or give your sincere opinion.

  budge [bʌdʒ] v. 움직이기 시작하다; 태도[견해]를 바꾸다
  If someone or something will not budge, they will not move.

* **dump** [dʌmp] vt. 내버리다, 쏟아 버리다
  If you dump something somewhere, you put it or unload it there quickly and carelessly.

* **scrape** [skreip] v. 문지르다, 긁어내다
  If you scrape something from a surface, you remove it, especially by pulling a sharp object over the surface.

* **mention** [ménʃən] vt. 말하다, 언급하다; n. 언급, 진술
  If you mention something, you say something about it, usually briefly.

  sonny [sʌ́ni] n. 애야, 얘, 아가 (소년에 대한 친근한 호칭)
  Some people address a boy or young man as sonny.

  toasty [tóusti] a. 따뜻하고 쾌적한; 토스트의
  If something is toasty, it is comfortably warm.

Vocabulary in Charlotte's Web

flibbertigibbet [flíbərtidʒìbit] n. 경박한 사람, 수다쟁이
Flibbertigibbet refers to a flighty or whimsical person, usually a young female.

hatch [hætʃ] v. (알이) 깨다, 부화하다; (음모·계획을) 꾸미다
When an egg hatches or when a bird, insect, or other animal hatches an egg, the egg breaks open and a baby comes out.

gosling [gázliŋ] n. 새끼 거위; 풋내기
A gosling is a baby goose.

woodpecker [wúdpèkər] n. 딱따구리
A woodpecker is a type of bird with a long sharp beak.

bitter [bítər] a. 신랄한, 통렬한; 쓴; n. 씀, 쓰라림 (bitterly ad. 쓰게, 따끔하게)
In a bitter argument or conflict, people argue very angrily or fight very fiercely.

by oneself idiom 혼자서, 외톨이로
By oneself means alone and without assistance, accompaniment, or help from others.

slant [slænt] v. 기울(게 하)다 a. 비스듬한, 기울어진; n. 경사, 비탈; (slanting a. 기울어진)
Something that slants is sloping, rather than horizontal or vertical.

stairway [stɛ́ərwèi] n. 계단
A stairway is a staircase or a flight of steps, inside or outside a building.

twirl [twəːrl] v. (손가락으로) 빙빙 꼬다; 빙빙 돌다, 회전하다; n. 회전, 선회
If you twirl something such as your hair, you twist it around your finger.

whisker [hwískər] n. 수염, 구레나룻
The whiskers of an animal such as a cat or a mouse are the long stiff hairs that grow near its mouth.

frolic [frálik] vi. 장난치며 놀다, 뛰놀다; n. 장난, 까불기
When people or animals frolic, they play or move in a lively, happy way.

merry [méri] a. 명랑한, 유쾌한, 즐거운
A merry sound or sight makes you feel cheerful.

4. Loneliness

avoid [əvɔ́id] vt. 피하다, 회피하다
If you avoid something unpleasant that might happen, you take action in order to prevent it from happening.

sour [sáuər] a. 심술궂은, (마음이) 비뚤어진; 신, 시큼한 (sourly ad. 심술궂게, 까다롭게)
Someone who is sour is bad-tempered and unfriendly.

gnaw [nɔː] v. 갉다, 갉아먹다
If people or animals gnaw something or gnaw at it, they bite it repeatedly.

spy [spai] v. 염탐하다; n. 스파이, 간첩
If you spy on someone, you watch them secretly.

glutton [glʌ́tn] n. 대식가, 폭식가
If you think that someone eats too much and is greedy, you can say he/she is a glutton.

creep [kriːp] vi. (crept–crept) 기다, 살금살금 걷다; n. 포복
When people or animals creep somewhere, they move quietly and slowly.

stealthy [stélθi] a. 몰래 하는, 남의 눈을 피하는, 비밀의 (stealthily ad. 몰래, 은밀히)
Stealthy actions or movements are performed quietly and carefully, so that no one will notice what you are doing.

private [práivit] a. 개인의, 사유의; 사적인; 비밀의
Your private things belong only to you, or may only be used by you.

crafty [krǽfti] a. 교활한, 간교한; 교묘한, 능란한
If you describe someone as crafty, you mean that they achieve what they want in a clever way, often by deceiving people.

cunning [kʌ́niŋ] n. 교활, 잔꾀; a. 교활한, 간사한
Cunning is the ability to achieve things in a clever way, often by deceiving other people.

abroad [əbrɔ́ːd] ad. 집 밖으로, 외출하여; 외국으로, 해외로
If you go abroad, you go outside of the house.

Vocabulary in Charlotte's Web

poke [pouk] v. 찌르다, 쑤시다, 들이대다; n. 찌름, 쑤심
If you poke someone or something, you quickly push them with your finger or with a sharp object.

underneath [ʌ̀ndərníːθ] prep. …의 아래에[지배하에]; ad. 아래에
If one thing is underneath another, it is directly under it, and may be covered or hidden by it.

cautious [kɔ́ːʃəs] a. 조심성 있는, 신중한 (cautiously ad. 조심스럽게)
Someone who is cautious acts very carefully in order to avoid possible danger.

dreary [dríəri] a. 적적한, 쓸쓸한, 음울한
If you describe something as dreary, you mean that it is dull and depressing.

soak [souk] v. 적시다, 빨아들이다; 젖다, 스며들다; n. 적심
If a liquid soaks something or if you soak something with a liquid, the liquid makes the thing very wet.

pour [pɔːr] v. 억수같이 퍼붓다; 흐르듯이 이동하다, 쇄도하다; 따르다, 쏟다
When it rains very heavily, you can say that it is pouring.

dejected [didʒéktid] a. 낙심[낙담]한, 풀 죽은
If you are dejected, you feel miserable or unhappy, especially because you have just been disappointed by something.

sulphur [sʌ́lfər] n. (= sulfur) 유황
Sulphur is a yellow chemical which has a strong smell.

molasses [məlǽsiz] n. 당밀(糖蜜)
Molasses is a thick, dark brown syrup which is produced when sugar is processed. It is used in cooking.

cud [kʌd] n. 새김질감 (반추 동물이 제1위에서 입으로 게워 내어 씹는 음식물)
When animals such as cows or sheep chew the cud, they slowly chew their partly-digested food over and over again in their mouth before finally swallowing it.

occasion [əkéiʒən] n. 경우, 특별한 일 (occasionally ad. 때때로, 가끔)
An occasion is a time when something happens, or a case of it happening.

4. Loneliness

* **rattle** [rǽtl] n. 덜거덕거리는 소리; v. 덜거덕거리며 움직이다
  A rattle is a short sharp knocking sound, when something is being shaken.

* **overhead** [óuvərhéd] ad. 머리 위에, 머리 위까지; a. 머리 위의, 머리 위를 통과하는
  You use overhead to indicate that something is above you or above the place that you are talking about.

 **Let's walk in the Book**

1. **Why did Wilbur find it difficult to sleep at night?**
   A. The other animals woke him up.
   B. Wilbur ate too much and felt ill.
   C. Wilbur's stomach was empty but his mind was full.
   D. Wilbur woke up from bad dreams.

2. **The oldest sheep said the quickest way to spoil a friendship is to _____**
   A. wake somebody up in the morning before he is ready.
   B. call out somebody's name in the middle of the night.
   C. cry about not having friends.
   D. be too loud at bedtime.

3. **Where was Charlotte's spider web?**
   A. It was in a barn window.
   B. It was outside of the pigpen next to the trough.
   C. It was on the top corner of the barn doorway.
   D. It was between the cracks in the fence surrounding the pigpen.

5. Charlotte

4. Why did Charlotte have problems seeing Wilbur?

A. Her eyes were too small.

B. She was near-sighted.

C. She was far-sighted.

D. She had bad eyes.

5. Put the following steps in order: What are the steps Charlotte follows to eat a fly? _____ - _____ - _____ - _____

A. Charlotte wraps the fly up.

B. Charlotte dives at the fly.

C. Charlotte drinks the fly's blood.

D. Charlotte knocks the fly out.

Vocabulary in Charlotte's Web

dozen [dʌ́zn] n. 상당히 많음; 1다스, 12개; a. 1다스의, 12(개)의
If you refer to dozens of things or people, you are emphasizing that there are very many of them.

barn [bɑːrn] n. (농가의) 헛간, 광
A large building on a farm in which hay and grain are kept.

midnight [mídnàit] n. 한밤중, 야반; a. 한밤중의, 야반의; 캄캄한
Midnight is used to describe something which happens or appears at midnight or in the middle of the night.

stirring [stə́ːriŋ] a. 활발한, 붐비는; 감동시키는, 고무하는
A stirring event or performance makes people very excited or enthusiastic.

racket [rǽkit] ① n. 떠드는 소리, 소음, 법석 ② n. 라켓
A racket is a loud unpleasant noise.

grind [graind] v. 갈다; 갈리다; 찧다, 빻다; n. 갈기, 빻기
If you grind something, you make it smooth or sharp by rubbing it against a hard surface.

clasher [klǽʃər] n. 이(빨)
clash (n. 땡땡 울리는 소리, 덜그렁덜그렁 부딪치는 소리) + -er (suf. …하는 것)

destroy [distrɔ́i] vt. 파괴하다; 멸하다; 망치다
To destroy something means to cause so much damage to it that it is completely ruined or does not exist any more.

property [prάpərti] n. 재산, 소유물; 소유권
Someone's property is all the things that belong to them or something that belongs to them.

decent [díːsənt] a. (사회 기준에) 맞는, 점잖은, 의젓한
Decent is used to describe something which is considered to be of an acceptable standard or quality.

chuckle [tʃʌ́kl] vi. 낄낄 웃다; n. 낄낄 웃음
When you chuckle, you laugh quietly.

5. Charlotte

whisper [hwíspər] v. 속삭이다, 작은 목소리로 말하다; n. 속삭임
When you whisper, you say something very quietly, using your breath rather than your throat.

cheat [tʃiːt] v. 속이다; 부정하다, 규칙[규정]을 어기다; n. 사기, 속임수
When someone cheats, they do not obey a set of rules which they should be obeying.

yawn [jɔːn] vi. 하품하다; n. 하품, 입을 크게 벌림
If you yawn, you open your mouth very wide and breathe in more air than usual, often when you are tired or when you are not interested in something.

dawn [dɔːn] n. 새벽, 동틀 녘; vi. 날이 새다, 밝아지다
Dawn is the time of day when light first appears in the sky, just before the sun rises.

doze [douz] v. 꾸벅꾸벅 졸다, 선잠을 자다; n. 졸기
If you doze off, you fall into a light sleep, especially during the daytime.

quit [kwit] v. 그만두다; 떠나다; (술·담배 등을) 끊다
If you quit an activity or quit doing something, you stop doing it.

errand [érənd] n. 심부름, 심부름 가기
An errand is a short trip that you make in order to do a job for someone, for example when you go to a shop to buy something for them.

weather-vane [wéðərvein] n. 풍향계
A weather-vane is a metal object on the roof of a building which turns round as the wind blows. It is used to show the direction of the wind.

faint [feint] a. 희미한, 어렴풋한; vi. 기절하다
A faint sound, color, mark, feeling, or quality has very little strength or intensity.

gleam [gliːm] n. 번득임; 어스레한 빛; vi. 어슴푸레 빛나다
If someone has a gleam in their eye, their eyes show a particular feeling.

tuck [tʌk] v. 밀어 넣다, 쑤셔 넣다; n. 접어 넣은 단
If you tuck something somewhere, you put it there so that it is safe, comfortable, or neat.

Vocabulary in Charlotte's Web

- **thorough** [θə́:rou] a. 철저한, 완전한, 빈틈없는 (thoroughly ad. 완전히, 철저히)
  A thorough action or activity is one that is done very carefully and in a detailed way so that nothing is forgotten.

- **ledge** [ledʒ] n. (벽·창 등에서 내민) 선반, 바위 턱
  A ledge is a narrow shelf along the bottom edge of a window.

- **ceiling** [sí:liŋ] n. 천장; 최고 한도
  A ceiling is the horizontal surface that forms the top part or roof inside a room.

- **mysterious** [mistíəriəs] a. 신비한, 불가사의한
  Someone or something that is mysterious is strange and is not known about or understood.

- **address** [ədrés] v. …에게 말을 걸다, 연설하다; n. 연설; 주소
  If you address someone or address a remark to them, you say something to them.

- **appropriate** [əpróuprièit] a. 적당한, 적절한; vt. 사용하다; 충당하다
  Something that is appropriate is suitable or acceptable for a particular situation.

- **signal** [sígnl] n. 신호; v. 신호를 보내다, 신호로 알리다
  A signal is a gesture, sound, or action which is intended to give a particular message to the person who sees or hears it.

- **blush** [blʌʃ] v. 얼굴을 붉히다, (얼굴이) 빨개지다; n. 얼굴을 붉힘, 홍조
  When you blush, your face becomes redder than usual because you are ashamed or embarrassed.

- **determine** [ditə́:rmin] v. 결심하다, 결정하다 (determined a. 결연한, 굳게 결심한)
  If you determine something, you decide it or settle it.

- **get in touch with (sb/sth)** idiom …와 연락하다, 접촉하다
  Make contact with somebody or something (by phone, letter, visit, etc.).

- **disgust** [disgʌ́st] n. 싫음, 혐오감; vt. 역겹게 하다, 넌더리나게 하다
  Disgust is a feeling of very strong dislike or disapproval.

5. Charlotte

‡ **nonsense** [nάnsens] n. 무의미한 말, 허튼소리; a. 무의미한, 어리석은
If you say that something spoken or written is nonsense, you mean that you consider it to be untrue or silly.

‡ **disturb** [distə́ːrb] v. 방해하다, 어지럽히다
If you disturb someone, you interrupt what they are doing and upset them.

‡‡ **spoil** [spɔil] v. 망치다, 못쓰게 만들다
If you spoil something, you prevent it from being successful or satisfactory.

‡‡ **beg** [beg] v. 구걸하다, 빌다; 간절히 바라다
If you beg someone to do something, you ask them very anxiously or eagerly to do it.

‡ **pardon** [pάːrdn] n. 용서, 허용; vt. 용서하다, 눈감아주다
You say 'I beg your pardon' or 'I do beg your pardon' as a way of apologizing for accidentally doing something wrong, such as disturbing someone or making a mistake.

* **objectionable** [əbdʒékʃənəbəl] a. 못마땅한, 싫은; 반대할 만한, 이의가 있는
If you describe someone or something as objectionable, you consider them to be extremely offensive and unacceptable.

‡ **meek** [miːk] a. 순한, 유순한, 온순한 (meekly ad. 온순하게)
If you describe a person as meek, you think that they are gentle and quiet, and likely to do what other people say.

복습 **manure** [mənjúər] n. 비료, 거름, 퇴비; vt. (땅에) 비료를[거름을] 주다
Manure is animal faeces, sometimes mixed with chemicals, that is spread on the ground in order to make plants grow healthy and strong.

복습 **slop** [slɑp] n. (돼지 사료용) 밥찌꺼기; 엎지름, 흙탕물; v. 엎지르다, 엎질러서 더럽히다
You can use slop or slops to refer to liquid waste containing the remains of food.

‡ **lick** [lik] v. 핥다; 스치다; 넘실거리다; n. 핥기
When people or animals lick something, they move their tongue across its surface.

Vocabulary in Charlotte's Web

gander [gǽndər] n. 거위의 수컷
A gander is a male goose.

waddle [wάdl] vi. 뒤뚱거리며 걷다, 어기적어기적 걷다
To walk with short steps, swinging the body from one side to the other.

salutation [sæ̀ljətéiʃən] n. 인사; (가벼운) 절, 경례
Salutation or a salutation is a greeting to someone.

greeting [grí:tiŋ] n. 인사, 경례, 환영의 말
A greeting is something friendly that you say or do when you meet someone.

fancy [fǽnsi] ① a. 장식적인, 화려한 ② n. 공상, 홀연히 내킨 생각; v. 공상하다
If you describe something as fancy, you mean that it is special, unusual, or elaborate.

silly [síli] a. 어리석은, 바보 같은, 시시한; n. 바보, 멍청이
If you say that someone or something is silly, you mean that they are foolish, childish, or ridiculous.

stretch [stretʃ] v. 퍼지다, 뻗어나다; 잡아 늘이다, 내뻗치다; n. 뻗침; 단숨
Something that stretches over an area or distance covers or exists in the whole of that area or distance.

gumdrop [gΛmdrὰp] n. (젤리 타입의) 캔디
A gumdrop is a chewy sweet which feels like firm rubber and usually tastes of fruit.

deny [dinái] vt. 부인[부정]하다; 거절하다
When you deny something, you state that it is not true.

flashy [flǽʃi] a. 속되게 번지르르한; 일시적으로 화려한, 섬광적인
If you describe a person or thing as flashy, you mean they are smart and noticeable, but in a rather vulgar way.

near-sighted [níərsáitid] a. 근시(안)의
Someone who is near-sighted cannot see distant things clearly.

5. Charlotte

‡ dreadful [drédfəl] a. 무서운, 두려운, 무시무시한 (dreadfully ad. 몹시; 무섭게)
Dreadful is used to emphasize the degree or extent of something bad.

복습 crawl [krɔːl] vi. 기어가다, 느릿느릿 가다; n. 기어감; 서행
When you crawl, you move forward on your hands and knees.

＊ blunder [blʌ́ndər] v. 걸려서 넘어질 뻔하다; 큰 실수를 하다, 일을 그르치다; n. 큰 실수
If you blunder somewhere, you move there in a clumsy and careless way.

＊ tangle [tǽŋgəl] v. 얽히게 하다; 엉키다; n. 엉킴; 혼란
If something is tangled or tangles, it becomes twisted together in an untidy way.

‡ thread [θred] n. 실, 바느질 실; vt. 실을 꿰다
Thread or a thread is a long very thin piece of a material such as cotton, nylon, or silk.

‡ furious [fjúəriəs] a. 맹렬한, 왕성한; 성난, 격노한 (furiously ad. 맹렬히)
Furious is also used to describe something that is done with great energy, effort, speed, or violence.

‡ dive [daiv] v. 뛰어들다, 돌진하다, 달려들다; n. 다이빙, 잠수
If you dive in a particular direction or into a particular place, you jump or move there quickly.

‡ plunge [plʌndʒ] v. 뛰어들다, 돌입하다; 내던지다; n. 돌진, 돌입
If something or someone plunges in a particular direction, they fall, rush, or throw themselves in that direction.

‡ rear [riər] a. 후방의; n. 뒤, 배후; 엉덩이 (rear end n. 엉덩이)
At or near the back of something.

＊ detest [ditést] vt. 몹시 싫어하다, 혐오하다
If you detest someone or something, you dislike them very much.

‡ gasp [gæsp] v. (놀람 따위로) 숨이 막히다, 헐떡거리다; n. 헐떡거림
When you gasp, you take a short quick breath through your mouth, especially when you are surprised, shocked, or in pain.

Vocabulary in Charlotte's Web

✱ **grasshopper** [grǽshàpər] n. 베짱이, 메뚜기
A grasshopper is an insect with long back legs that jumps high into the air and makes a high, vibrating sound.

✱ **beetle** [bíːtl] n. 갑충(甲蟲), 딱정벌레
A beetle is an insect with a hard covering to its body.

✱ **moth** [mɔ(ː)θ] n. 나방
A moth is an insect like a butterfly which usually flies about at night.

cockroach [kákròutʃ] n. 바퀴(벌레)
A cockroach is a large brown insect that is sometimes found in warm places or where food is kept.

★ **gnat** [næt] n. [곤충] 각다귀 (피를 빨아 먹는 작은 곤충)
A gnat is a very small flying insect that bites people and usually lives near water.

midge [midʒ] n. (모기·각다귀 등의) 작은 날벌레
Midges are very small insects which bite.

daddy longlegs [dǽdi lɔ́ːŋlègz] n. 소경거미, 꾸정모기
A daddy longlegs is a flying insect with very long legs.

centipede [séntəpìːd] n. 지네
A centipede is a long, thin creature with a lot of legs.

✱ **cricket** [kríkit] n. 귀뚜라미
A cricket is a small jumping insect that produces short, loud sounds by rubbing its wings together.

✱ **trap** [træp] n. 덫, 함정; v. 덫을 놓다, 함정에 빠뜨리다 (trapper n. 덫을 놓는 사람)
A trap is a device which is placed somewhere or a hole which is dug somewhere in order to catch animals or birds.

복습 **miserable** [mízərəbəl] a. 불쌍한, 비참한, 딱한, 가엾은
Something that is miserable is very unhappy or uncomfortable.

✱ **inheritance** [inhéritəns] n. 상속, 계승; 유산
Your inheritance is the particular characteristics or qualities which your family or ancestors had and which you are born with.

5. Charlotte

* **gloomy** [glú:mi] a. 우울한; 어두운, 음침한
  If people are gloomy, they are unhappy and have no hope.

  bloodthirsty [blʌ́dθə̀:rsti] a. 피에 굶주린, 살벌한, 잔인한
  Bloodthirsty people are eager to use violence or display a strong interest in violent things.

* **clever** [klévər] a. 영리한, 똑똑한; 손재주 있는
  Someone who is clever is intelligent and able to understand things easily or plan things well.

* **cruel** [krú:əl] a. 잔혹한, 잔인한, 무자비한
  A situation or event that is cruel is very harsh and causes people distress.

* **intend** [inténd] v. 의도하다; …할 작정이다
  If you intend to do something, you have decided or planned to do it.

* **wit** [wit] n. 기지, 재치; 지혜, 지력, 이해력
  Wit is the ability to use words or ideas in an amusing, clever, and imaginative way.

* **multiply** [mʌ́ltəplài] v. 늘리다, 증가하다; (수를) 곱하다
  When animals and insects multiply, they increase in number by giving birth to large numbers of young.

* **numerous** [njú:mərəs] a. 다수의, 수많은
  If people or things are numerous, they exist or are present in large numbers.

  wipe out phrasal v. 무찌르다, 전멸하다
  To wipe out something such as a place or a group of people or animals means to destroy them completely.

* **plot** [plɑt] v. 몰래 꾸미다, 계획하다, 음모하다; n. 음모, 계획; 줄거리
  If people plot to do something or plot something that is illegal or wrong, they plan secretly to do it.

* **feather** [féðər] n. (pl.) 깃털, 깃
  A bird's feathers are the soft covering on its body.

Vocabulary in Charlotte's Web

* **excitement** [iksáitmənt] n. 흥분 (상태)
You use excitement to refer to the state of being excited, or to something that excites you.

* **clover** [klóuvər] n. 토끼풀
Clover is a small plant with pink or white ball-shaped flowers.

* **gamble** [gǽmbəl] n. 도박, 노름; 모험; v. 노름[도박]을 하다, 내기를 하다
A gamble is a risky action or decision that you take in the hope of gaining money, success, or an advantage over other people.

* **fierce** [fiərs] a. 사나운, 흉포한; 맹렬한
A fierce animal or person is very aggressive or angry.

* **brutal** [brú:tl] a. 잔인한, 야만적인; 모진, 혹독한
A brutal act or person is cruel and violent.

* **scheme** [ski:m] n. 계획; 음모; v. 계획을 세우다; 음모를 꾸미다
(scheming a. 교활한, 흉계가 있는)
A scheme is someone's plan for achieving something.

* **mere** [miər] a. 단순한, 순전한, 단지 …에 불과한 (merely ad. 단지, 다만)
You use mere to emphasize how unimportant or inadequate something is, in comparison to the general situation you are describing.

* **doubt** [daut] n. 의심, 회의; 불신; v. 의심하다, 수상히 여기다
If you have doubt or doubts about something, you feel uncertain about it and do not know whether it is true or possible.

* **discover** [diskʌ́vər] vt. …을 알다, 깨닫다; 발견하다
If you discover something that you did not know about before, you become aware of it or learn of it.

* **bold** [bould] a. 대담한, 과감한; 뻔뻔스러운
Someone who is bold is not afraid to do things which involve risk or danger.

* **exterior** [ikstíəriər] n. 외부, 외면; a. 외부의, 밖의
You can refer to someone's usual appearance or behavior as their exterior.

5. Charlotte

prove [pru:v] v. …임이 알려지다; 입증[증명]하다; 시험하다
If something proves to be true, it becomes clear after a period of time that it is true.

loyal [lɔ́iəl] a. 충성스러운, 성실한, 충실한
Someone who is loyal remains firm in their friendship or support for a person or thing.

Let's walk in the Book

1. Why did Fern visit the farm almost every day in Summer?
   A. She had less school homework.
   B. She had to help her uncle on the farm.
   C. The weather was nicer in the spring.
   D. School was over.

2. What did Mr. Zuckerman do on the first week of July?
   A. He cut all the tall grass from the field.
   B. He took the horses out to ride through the fields.
   C. He collected the apples from the orchard.
   D. He cleaned the barn.

3. What did both Fern and Avery like to do in the springtime?
   A. They liked to play in the hay.
   B. They liked to watch the animals in the barn together.
   C. They liked to chew on potato vines.
   D. They liked to help Mr. Zuckerman do farm work.

4. After the goose herself, who was the next animal who knew the goslings arrived?
   A. Templeton
   B. Wilbur
   C. Charlotte
   D. The Gander

6. Summer Days

5. Why did all of the animals look at Templeton when the goslings hatched?

A. Templeton started an argument the gander.

B. Templeton was not trusted or well liked by the animals.

C. Templeton surprised the animals when said congratulations.

D. Templeton tried to steal a gosling.

Vocabulary in Charlotte's Web

lilac [láilək] n. 라일락; 엷은 자색
A lilac or a lilac tree is a small tree which has sweet-smelling purple, pink, or white flowers in large, cone-shaped groups.

trout [traut] n. 송어
A trout is a fairly large fish that lives in rivers and streams.

brook [bruk] ① n. 시내, 개천 ② vt. 견디다, 참다
A brook is a small stream.

stiff [stif] a. 뻣뻣한, 딱딱한; 완강한, 완고한
Something that is stiff is firm or does not bend easily.

hitch [hitʃ] v. 걸다, 매다; 홱 움직이다; n. 급정지
If you hitch something to something else, you hook it or fasten it there.

mow [mou] v. 베다, 베어내다
If you mow an area of grass, you cut it using a machine called a lawn-mower.

swathe [sweið] n. 붕대, 감싸는 천; vt. 감다, 싸다
A swathe of cloth is a long strip of cloth, especially one that is wrapped around someone or something.

thunder [θʌ́ndər] n. 우레, 뇌성, 천둥; vi. 천둥치다; 큰 소리를 내다
(thunder shower : 번개가 따르는 소낙비)
Thunder is the loud noise that you hear from the sky after a flash of lightning, especially during a storm.

rake [reik] v. 갈퀴질하다, 긁다; n. 갈퀴, 써레; 부지깽이
If you rake a surface, you move a rake across it in order to make it smooth and level.

pitch [pitʃ] v. 던지다; 처박다
If you pitch something somewhere, you throw it with quite a lot of force.

haul [hɔːl] v. 운반하다, 차로 나르다; 세게 잡아끌다; n. 끌기, 견인; 운반
If you haul something which is heavy or difficult to move, you move it using a lot of effort.

6. Summer Days

‡ wagon [wǽgən] n. 짐마차, 4륜 마차; v. 짐마차로 여행[수송·운반]하다
A wagon is a container on wheels.

* hoist [hɔist] vt. 올리다, 높이 달다, 끌어올리다; n. 감아올리기
If something heavy is hoisted somewhere, it is lifted there using a machine such as a crane.

‡ loft [lɔ:ft] n. (짚·건초 등을 저장하는) 다락; 지붕 밑의 방
A loft is the space inside the sloping roof of a house or other building, where things are sometimes stored.

timothy [tíməθi] n. 큰조아재비 (볏과의 목초)
A grass grown for hay.

* jubilee [dʒú:bəlì:] n. 축제, 축전; 50[25]년제
A jubilee is a special anniversary of an event, especially the 25th or 50th anniversary.

‡ swamp [swɑmp] n. 늪, 습지; v. 궁지에 빠뜨리다; 가라앉다
A swamp is an area of very wet land with wild plants growing in it.

‡ sparrow [spǽrou] n. 참새
A sparrow is a small brown bird which is common in towns and cities.

‡ bough [bau] n. 큰 가지
A bough is a large branch of a tree.

phoebe [fí:bi] n. 딱새 무리의 작은 새 (미국산)
A phoebe is a small dun-colored North American flycatcher.

teeter [tí:tər] v. 흔들리다, 비틀거리며 나가다
If someone or something teeters, they shake in an unsteady way, and seem to be about to lose their balance and fall over.

* wag [wæg] v. 흔들다, 흔들어 움직이다; 흔들거리다
When a dog wags its tail, it repeatedly waves its tail from side to side.

‡ brief [bri:f] a. 잠시[잠깐]의; 간결한; n. 개요; 짧은 보고; vt. 간단히 알리다, 요약하다
Something that is brief lasts for only a short time.

Vocabulary in Charlotte's Web

* **interlude** [íntərlùːd] n. 간주곡; 막간(극 · 여흥); (시간과 시간의) 사이, 중간
  An interlude is a short period of time when an activity or situation stops and something else happens.

* **swoop** [swuːp] v. 내리 덮치다, 달려들다; 급강하하다
  When a bird or airplane swoops, it suddenly moves downwards through the air in a smooth curving movement.

‡ **scold** [skould] v. 꾸짖다, 잔소리하다
  If you scold someone, you speak angrily to them because they have done something wrong.

* **dandelion** [dǽndəlàiən] n. [식물] 민들레
  A dandelion is a wild plant which has yellow flowers with lots of thin petals.

‡ **stem** [stem] n. 줄기, 대
  The stem of a plant is the thin, upright part on which the flowers and leaves grow.

nectar [néktər] n. 과즙, 화밀(花蜜)
  Nectar is a sweet liquid produced by flowers, which bees and other insects collect.

Frigidaire [frìdʒədɛ̀ər] n. 전기 냉장고 (상표명)
  Frigidaire is a major appliance company in the US.

‡ **spit** [spit] n. 침, 거품; v. 뱉다, 토해내다, 뿜어내다
  Spit is the watery liquid produced in your mouth.

복습 **weed** [wiːd] n. 잡초; v. 잡초를 없애다, 김매다
  A weed is a wild plant that grows in gardens or fields of crops and prevents the plants that you want from growing properly.

* **stalk** [stɔːk] ① n. 줄기, 대; 잎자루 ② v. 몰래 접근하다; 가만히 뒤를 밟다; 젠체하며 걷다
  The stalk of a flower, leaf, or fruit is the thin part that joins it to the plant or tree.

복습 **poke** [pouk] v. 찌르다, 쑤시다, 들이대다; n. 찌름, 쑤심
  If you poke someone or something, you quickly push them with your finger or with a sharp object.

6. Summer Days

worm [wəːrm] n. (꿈틀거리며 기어 다니는) 벌레; v. 꿈틀꿈틀 나아가다; 서서히 나아가게 하다
A worm is a small animal with a long thin body, no bones and no legs.

vine [vain] n. 덩굴 식물; 포도나무
Any climbing plant with long thin stems.

cramped [kræmpt] a. ① 비좁은, 갑갑한; 읽기 어려운 ② 경련을 일으킨
Not having room to move freely.

shell [ʃel] n. 껍질, 조가비; 포탄
The shell of a nut or egg is the hard covering which surrounds it.

anxious [ǽŋkʃəs] a. 갈망하는; 걱정하는
If you are anxious to do something or anxious that something should happen, you very much want to do it or very much want it to happen.

announcement [ənáunsmənt] n. 공고, 고시, 발표
The announcement of something that has happened is the act of telling people about it.

gratify [grǽtəfài] vt. 만족시키다, 기쁘게 하다
If you are gratified by something, it gives you pleasure or satisfaction.

unremitting [ʌ̀nrimítiŋ] a. 끊임없는, 끈기 있는, 꾸준히 노력하는
Something that is unremitting continues without stopping or becoming less intense.

effort [éfərt] n. 노력, 수고
If you make an effort to do something, you try very hard to do it.

patience [péiʃəns] n. 인내, 인내심, 참을성
If you have patience, you are able to stay calm and not get annoyed.

sincere [sinsíər] a. 성실한, 참된, 진실의
If you say that someone is sincere, you approve of them because they really mean the things they say.

dud [dʌd] n. 실패, 쓸모없는 것; 불발탄
Dud means not working properly or not successful.

Vocabulary in Charlotte's Web

* **bead** [biːd] n. 구슬, 유리알; 방울; vt. 구슬로 장식하다 (beady a. 구슬 같은)
  Beads are small pieces of colored glass, wood, or plastic with a hole through the middle.

* **pound** [paund] v. 마구 치다[두드리다], 연타[난타]하다; 맹포격하다; n. 타격, 연타
  If you pound something or pound on it, you hit it with great force, usually loudly and repeatedly.

‡ **moral** [mɔ́(ː)rəl] n. 도덕, 품행; 교훈; a. 도덕적인, 정신적인
  Morals are principles and beliefs concerning right and wrong behavior.

‡ **conscience** [kánʃəns] n. 양심, 도의심; 선악의 판단력
  Your conscience is the part of your mind that tells you whether what you are doing is right or wrong.

* **scruple** [skrúːpəl] n. 양심의 가책; 주저, 망설임; v. 망설이다, 양심의 가책을 받다
  Scruples are moral principles or beliefs that make you unwilling to do something that seems wrong.

* **decency** [díːsnsi] n. 품위, 체면, 예의, 예절
  Decency is the quality of following accepted moral standards.

milk of (human) kindness idiom 타고난[자연스러운] 인정 (Shakespeare의 Macbeth에서)
  Kind behavior, considered to be natural to human beings.

rodent [róudənt] n. (쥐·다람쥐 등의) 설치 동물; a. 갉아거리는; 설치류의
  Rodents are small mammals which have sharp front teeth. Rats, mice, and squirrels are rodents.

compunction [kəmpʌ́ŋkʃən] n. 양심의 가책, 후회, 회한
  A feeling of guilt or anxiety about something you have done or might do.

‡ **bill** [bil] ① n. (가늘고 납작한) 부리 ② n. 계산서, 청구서; 지폐
  A bird's bill is its beak.

* **appall** [əpɔ́ːl] vt. 오싹하게[질겁하게] 하다
  If something appalls you, it disgusts you because it seems so bad or unpleasant.

6. Summer Days

junky [dʒʌ́ŋki] a. 허섭스레기의; 2급 품의
If you describe something as junky, you think it is of poor quality or of little value.

‡ mutter [mʌ́tər] v. 중얼거리다; 불평하다; n. 중얼거림; 불평
If you mutter, you speak very quietly so that you cannot easily be heard, often because you are complaining about something.

★ tinkle [tíŋkəl] v. 딸랑딸랑 울리다; n. 딸랑딸랑 (소리) (tinkling a. 딸랑딸랑 울리는)
If something tinkles, it makes a clear, high-pitched, ringing noise, especially as small parts of it strike a surface.

‡ ancient [éinʃənt] a. 오래된; 고대의; 먼 옛날의; n. 고대인
Ancient means very old, or having existed for a long time.

untenable [ʌnténəbəl] a. 지지할 수 없는, 이치가 닿지 않는
An argument, theory, or position that is untenable cannot be defended successfully against criticism or attack.

‡ rot [rɑt] v. 썩(이)다, 못쓰게 만들다; n. 썩음, 부패 (rotten a. 썩은)
When food, wood, or another substance rots, or when something rots it, it becomes softer and is gradually destroyed.

★ stink [stíŋk] v. 고약한 냄새가 나다, 악취가 풍기다; n. 악취
If you say that something stinks, you mean that you disapprove of it because it involves ideas, feelings, or practices that you do not like.

★ snarl [snɑːrl] v. 으르렁거리다; 고함[호통]치다; n. 으르렁거림
When an animal snarls, it makes a deep rough sound in its throat while showing its teeth.

nudge [nʌdʒ] v. 슬쩍 찌르다, 조금씩[슬쩍] 움직이다; 주의를 환기시키다
If you nudge someone or something into a place or position, you gently push them there.

lair [lɛər] n. (들짐승의) 굴, 집; 은신처, 잠복처
A lair is a place where a wild animal lives, usually a place which is underground or well-hidden.

Let's walk in the Book

1. Why did the animals hate flies?

A. Flies pestered the animals.

B. Flies ate the animals' food.

C. Flies said rude things to the animals.

D. Flies complained often.

7. Bad News

2. What made Wilbur happy about the way Charlotte ate flies?

   A. Charlotte wrapped the fly up.

   B. Charlotte ate the flies quickly.

   C. Charlotte put the fly to sleep before eating it.

   D. Charlotte talked to the fly before eating it.

3. What did the oldest sheep notice about Wilbur's appearance?

   A. The old sheep saw that Wilbur was getting fatter.

   B. The old sheep saw that Wilbur was getting longer.

   C. The old sheep saw that Wilbur was getting stronger.

   D. The old sheep saw that Wilbur was changing color.

4. The old sheep said that young pigs got killed _____

   A. at the end of the summer.

   B. when the leaves changed color.

   C. when the really cold weather came.

   D. at the end of the winter.

5. According to the oldest sheep, who was NOT in on the conspiracy to kill Wilber?

   A. Mr. Zuckerman

   B. Mr. Arable

   C. Lurvy

   D. Fern

Vocabulary in Charlotte's Web

campaign [kæmpéin] n. (일련의) 행동, 캠페인
A campaign is a planned set of activities that people carry out over a period of time.

pester [péstər] vt. 괴롭히다, 못살게 굴다, 고통을 주다; n. 훼방, 방해
If you say that someone is pestering you, you mean that they keep asking you to do something, or keep talking to you, and you find this annoying.

loathe [louð] vt. 몹시 싫어하다; 지겨워하다, 질색하다
If you loathe something or someone, you dislike them very much.

admire [ædmáiər] v. 감탄하다, 탄복하다
If you admire someone or something, you like and respect them very much.

victim [víktim] n. 희생(자)
A victim is someone who has been hurt or killed.

anaesthetic [ænəsθétik] n. (= anaesthetic) 마취제; a. 마취의; 무감각한
Anaesthetic is a substance that doctors use to stop you feeling pain during an operation.

throw in phrasal v. 덤으로 주다
If a person or business selling goods throws something in, they provide it for free when you buy something else from them.

gain [gein] v. 얻다, 획득하다; 증가하다; 이익을 얻다; n. 이익
If a person or place gains something such as an ability or quality, they gradually get more of it.

fatten [fǽtn] v. 살찌우다, 기름지게 하다
If an animal is fattened, or if it fattens, it becomes fatter as a result of eating more.

stool [stu:l] n. (등이 없는) 걸상; 발판(대)
A seat without any support for the back or arms.

rigid [rídʒid] a. 단단한; 엄격한, 완고한
If someone goes rigid, their body becomes very straight and stiff, usually as a result of shock or fear.

7. Bad News

* **conspiracy** [kənspírəsi] n. 음모, 공모
  A conspiracy is an agreement between a group of people which other people think is wrong or is likely to be harmful.

* **butcher** [bútʃər] vt. 도살[학살]하다; n. 고깃간 주인, 도살업자, 학살자
  To butcher an animal means to kill it and cut it up for meat.

  .22 [twenti-tu:] n. 22구경 라이플[권총]

* **race** [reis] v. 질주하다, 경주하다; n. 경주; 급히 서두름
  To move very fast; To move somebody or something very fast.

* **pluck** [plʌk] ① v. 잡아 뜯다, 뽑다; n. 잡아 뜯기 ② n. 담력, 용기
  If you pluck something from somewhere, you take it between your fingers and pull it sharply from where it is.

* **burst** [bə:rst] v. 갑자기 …하다; 파열하다, 터지다; n. 파열, 돌발
  If you burst into tears, laughter, or song, you suddenly begin to cry, laugh, or sing.

* **moan** [moun] v. 신음하다, 끙끙대다; n. 신음
  If you moan, you make a low sound, usually because you are unhappy or in pain.

* **snap** [snæp] v. 날카롭게[느닷없이] 말하다; 휙 잡다, 짤깍 소리 내다; n. 툭 소리 냄
  If someone snaps at you, they speak to you in a sharp, unfriendly way.

* **brisk** [brisk] a. 활발한, 팔팔한 (briskly ad. 활발하게, 힘차게)
  A brisk activity or action is done quickly and in an energetic way.

  hysteric [histérik] n. 히스테리의 발작; 히스테리성의 사람
  If someone is in hysterics or is having hysterics, they are in a state of uncontrolled excitement, anger, or panic.

 **Let's walk in the Book**

1. **When did Fern tell her parents about the animals at Mr. Zuckerman's farm?**

   A. On a Sunday morning at breakfast.

   B. On a Saturday afternoon at lunchtime.

   C. On a weekday morning before school.

   D. On a Sunday evening at dinnertime.

2. **Who did Fern say was Wilbur's best friend?**

   A. Templeton

   B. The Goose

   C. The Goslings

   D. Charlotte

3. **Where did Fern need to go after eating?**

   A. She needed to go to Mr. Zuckerman's farm.

   B. She needed to do her chores around the house.

   C. She needed to go to the market.

   D. She needed to go to Sunday school.

4. **Why was Mrs. Arable concerned about Fern?**

   A. She was concerned that Fern was spending too much time at Mr. Zuckerman's farm and not doing enough work at home.

   B. She was concerned that Fern saw Wilbur as a pet rather than a pig on a farm.

8. A Talk at Home

C. She was concerned that Fern spoke to the animals on the farm.

D. She was concerned that Fern was becoming a nuisance for Mr. Zuckerman because of all the time she spent on the farm.

5. Mr. Arable thought that _____

A. Fern should see a doctor.

B. animals didn't talk.

C. Mrs. Arable should not worry about Fern.

D. Fern was acting strangely.

Vocabulary in Charlotte's Web

slingshot [slíŋʃàt] n. 새총
A slingshot is a device for shooting small stones.

queer [kwiər] a. 언짢은; 별난, 기묘한; 수상한
Something that is queer is strange.

cellar [sélər] n. 지하실, 지하층
A cellar is a room underneath a building, which is often used for storing things in.

nod [nɑd] v. 끄덕이다, 끄덕여 표시하다; n. 끄덕임 (동의 · 인사 · 신호 · 명령)
If you nod, you move your head downwards and upwards to show agreement, understanding, or approval.

suck [sʌk] v. 빨다, 빨아들이다, 흡수하다; n. 빨기
If you suck something, you hold it in your mouth and pull at it with the muscles in your cheeks and tongue.

adore [ədɔ́ːr] vt. 아주 좋아하다, 숭배하다
If you adore someone, you feel great love and admiration for them.

vague [veig] a. 어렴풋한, 막연한 (vaguely ad. 모호하게, 막연하게)
If something written or spoken is vague, it does not explain or express things clearly.

faint [feint] a. 희미한, 어렴풋한; vi. 기절하다
A faint sound, color, mark, feeling, or quality has very little strength or intensity.

stick [stik] ① v. (stuck-stuck) 찌르다, 찔러 넣다; 고수[고집]하다; n. 한 번 찌름 ② n. 막대기, 지팡이
If you stick something somewhere, you put it there in a rather casual way.

ramble on phrasal v. 오랫동안 이야기하다
If you say that someone is rambling on, you mean that they have been talking for a long time in a boring and rather confused way.

pretend [priténd] v. …인 체하다, 가장하다
If you pretend that something is the case, you act in a way that is intended to make people believe that it is the case, although in fact it is not.

8. A Talk at Home

‡ wonder [wʌ́ndər] vi. 호기심을 가지다; 경탄하다; n. 경탄할 만한 것, 경이

If you wonder about something, you think about it, either because it interests you and you want to know more about it, or because you are worried or suspicious about it.

‡ imagination [imæ̀dʒənéiʃən] n. 상상(력)

Your imagination is the part of your mind which allows you to form pictures or ideas of things that do not necessarily exist in real life.

‡ grin [grin] v. 이를 드러내고 싱긋 웃다; n. 싱긋 웃음

When you grin, you smile broadly.

 **Let's walk in the Book**

1. How did Wilbur boast to Charlotte?
   A. He said he could spin a better web than Charlotte.
   B. He said his legs were more useful than Charlotte's.
   C. He said his legs were hairier than Charlotte's.
   D. He said he could spin a web if he tried.

2. How did Charlotte feel when she saw Wilbur trying to spin a web?
   A. She was proud of Wilbur because he was not a quitter.
   B. She was embarrassed because Wilbur thought he could spin a web.
   C. She was afraid that Wilbur might hurt himself.
   D. She was happy that Wilbur was embarrassing himself.

3. Where did Wilbur want to be that evening?
   A. He wanted to be at Fern's house eating nuts and berries.
   B. He wanted to be in the forest searching and sniffing on the ground.
   C. He wanted to be by the brook drinking the fresh water.
   D. He wanted to be by the orchard eating apples.

9. Wilbur's Boast

4. Why was Charlotte glad she was a sedentary spider?

A. Rushing around looking for a good thing was exciting.

B. Waiting for what came to her web gave her a chance to think.

C. Making a web and waiting gave her a lot of time to sleep.

D. She knew her web was a safe place and didn't want to wander away from it.

5. How did the lamb hurt Wilbur's feelings?

A. The lamb called Wilbur fat.

B. The lamb said that Wilbur smelled bad.

C. The lamb said that Wilbur was the ugliest animal on the farm.

D. The lamb told Wilbur that he would be killed in the winter.

Vocabulary in Charlotte's Web

✽ **boast** [boust] n. 자랑(거리), 허풍; v. 자랑하다
If someone boasts about something that they have done or that they own, they talk about it very proudly.

✽ **delicate** [délikət] a. 섬세한, 고운, 우아한; 예민한; 미묘한
Something that is delicate is small and beautifully shaped.

strand [strænd] ① n. 가닥, 외가닥으로 꼰 끈 ② v. 좌초시키다; 오도 가도 못하다
A strand of something such as hair, wire, or thread is a single thin piece of it.

✽ **weave** [wi:v] v. (wove-woven) (직물을) 짜다, 엮다
If you weave cloth or a carpet, you make it by crossing threads over and under each other.

✽ **witness** [wítnis] v. 목격하다, 보다; 입증하다; n. 목격자; 증거
If you witness something, you see it happen.

coxa [káksə] n. 고관절, 엉덩이
The coxa is the basal segment of a limb of various arthropods.

trochanter [troukǽntər] n. [곤충] 전절(轉節) (발의 제 2관절)
The trochanter is a bony bump on the femur to which large muscles are attached.

femur [fí:mər] n. [곤충] 퇴절(腿節); 넓적다리
Your femur is the large bone in the upper part of your leg.

patella [pətélə] n. [곤충] 기관부(基關部); 무릎뼈, 슬개골
The patella is a kneecap.

tibia [tíbiə] n. [곤충] 경절(脛節); 경골, 정강이뼈
Your tibia is the inner bone of the two bones in the lower part of your leg.

metatarsus [mètətá:rsəs] n. [곤충] 기부절(基附節), 윗발목마디
The metatarsus is the second leg segment from the end, between the tibia and tarsus.

tarsus [tá:rsəs] n. [곤충] 부절(跗節), 다리 앞쪽 끝마디
The tarsus is the part of the foot of a vertebrate between the metatarsus and the leg.

9. Wilbur's Boast

chubby [tʃʌ́bi] a. 토실토실 살찐, 통통한
A chubby person is rather fat.

chuckle [tʃʌ́kl] vi. 낄낄 웃다; n. 낄낄 웃음
When you chuckle, you laugh quietly.

coach [koutʃ] v. 지도하다, 코치하다, 가르치다; n. 마차; 장거리 버스; 코치
If you coach someone, you give them special teaching in a particular subject.

scramble [skrǽmbəl] v. 기어오르다; 서로 (다투어) 빼앗다; n. 기어오르기
If you scramble over rocks or up a hill, you move quickly over them or up it using your hands to help you.

manure [mənjúər] n. 비료, 거름, 퇴비; vt. (땅에) 비료를[거름을] 주다
Manure is animal faeces, sometimes mixed with chemicals, that is spread on the ground in order to make plants grow healthy and strong.

spinneret [spínərèt] n. (거미·누에 등의) 방적 돌기 (실이 나오는 구멍)
A spinneret is a spider's silk-spinning organ.

hurl [həːrl] v. 세게 내던지다, 집어던지다
If you hurl something, you throw it violently and with a lot of force.

dragline [drǽglain] n. (기구 등의) 끄는 줄, 유도 로프
A dragline is a rope used to guide the movement of the load of a crane.

hesitate [hézətèit] v. 주저하다, 머뭇거리다, 망설이다
If you hesitate, you do not speak or act for a short time, usually because you are uncertain, embarrassed, or worried about what you are going to say or do.

glance [glæns] v. 흘긋 보다, 잠깐 보다; n. 흘긋 봄, 일견
If you glance at something or someone, you look at them very quickly and then look away again immediately.

hasty [héisti] a. 급한, 신속한 (hastily ad. 급히, 서둘러서)
A hasty movement, action, or statement is sudden, and often done in reaction to something that has just happened.

Vocabulary in Charlotte's Web

rear [riər] n. 엉덩이; 뒤, 배후; a. 후방의
The part of the body that you sit on.

thump [θʌmp] n. 탁, 쿵 (소리); v. 탁 치다, 부딪치다
The sound of something heavy hitting the ground or another object.

grunt [grʌnt] vi. (돼지가) 꿀꿀거리다; (사람이) 툴툴거리다; n. 꿀꿀[툴툴]거리는 소리
When an animal grunts, it makes a low rough noise.

sway [swei] v. 흔들리다; 동요하다; n. 동요, 지배
When people or things sway, they lean or swing slowly from one side to the other.

recover [rikʌvər] v. 회복하다; 되찾다, 원상태로 되다
When you recover from an illness or an injury, you become well again.

bump [bʌmp] n. 충돌; 혹; v. 부딪치다, 충돌하다; 마주치다
A bump is a minor injury or swelling that you get if you bump into something or if something hits you.

oblige [əbláidʒ] v. 은혜를 베풀다; 강요하다
To oblige someone means to be helpful to them by doing what they have asked you to do.

creep [kri:p] vi. (crept-crept) 기다, 살금살금 걷다; n. 포복
When people or animals creep somewhere, they move quietly and slowly.

crouch [krautʃ] v. 몸을 구부리다, 쭈그리다, 웅크리다; n. 웅크림
If you are crouching, your legs are bent under you so that you are close to the ground and leaning forward slightly.

curl [kə:rl] n. 컬, 곱슬머리; vt. 곱슬곱슬하게 하다 (curly a. 곱슬곱슬한)
If you have curls, your hair is in the form of tight curves and spirals.

seize [si:z] v. 잡다, 붙들다, 붙잡다; 이해하다
To take somebody or something in your hand suddenly and using force.

fond [fɑnd] a. 좋아하는, 정다운, 다정한
(be fond of idiom …을 좋아하다, …이 좋다)
If you are fond of someone, you feel affection for them.

9. Wilbur's Boast

stale [steil] a. (음식 따위가) 상한, 신선하지 않은
Stale food is no longer fresh or good to eat.

quit [kwit] v. 그만두다; 떠나다; (술·담배 등을) 끊다 (quitter n. 포기하는 사람)
If you quit an activity or quit doing something, you stop doing it.

willing [wíliŋ] a. 기꺼이…하는
If someone is willing to do something, they are fairly happy about doing it and will do it if they are asked or required to do it.

summon [sʌ́mən] vt. 내다, 불러 일으키다; 소환하다, 호출하다
If you summon a quality, you make a great effort to have it.

trail [treil] v. 끌다, 추적하다; n. 끌고 간 자국, 흔적
If you trail something or it trails, it hangs down loosely behind you as you move along.

neglect [niglékt] vt. 무시하다, 간과하다; 게을리 하다, 소홀히 하다; n. 태만, 소홀, 무시
If you neglect someone or something, you fail to look after them properly.

fasten [fǽsn] v. 묶다, 죄다; 닫히다
When you fasten something, you close it by means of buttons or a strap, or some other device.

thud [θʌd] n. 쿵, 털썩, 덜컥 (무거운 물건이 떨어지는 소리)
A thud is a dull sound, such as that which a heavy object makes when it hits something soft.

advise [ædváiz] v. 충고하다, 조언하다; 의논하다, 상담하다
If you advise someone to do something, you tell them what you think they should do.

lack [læk] v. …이 없다, …이 결핍되다; n. 부족
If you say that someone or something lacks a particular quality or that a particular quality is lacking in them, you mean that they do not have any or enough of it.

sigh [sai] v. 한숨 쉬다; n. 한숨, 탄식
When you sigh, you let out a deep breath, as a way of expressing feelings such as disappointment, tiredness, or pleasure.

Vocabulary in Charlotte's Web

Queensborough Bridge n. New Westminster에 있는 다리

‡ starve [stɑːrv] v. 굶주리다, 굶어 죽다; 갈망하다
If people starve, they suffer greatly from lack of food which sometimes leads to their death.

* trot [trɑt] v. 빠른 걸음으로 가다; 총총걸음 치다; n. 빠른 걸음
If you trot somewhere, you move fairly fast at a speed between walking and running, taking small quick step.

back and forth idiom 앞뒤로, 이리저리
If you move back and forth, you move from one place to another and back again repeatedly.

* sedentary [sédəntèri] a. 앉아 있는; 정주하는; n. 앉아서 일하는 사람, 늘 앉아 있는 사람
Someone who has a sedentary lifestyle or job sits down a lot of the time and does not take much exercise.

beechnut [bíːtʃnʌt] n. 너도밤나무 열매
Beechnuts are small sweet triangular nut of various beech trees.

truffle [trʌfəl] n. 송로(松露)·알버섯과의 버섯)의 일종
A truffle is a round type of fungus which is expensive and considered very good to eat.

delectable [diléktəbəl] a. 맛있는; 즐거운, 기쁜
If you describe something, especially food or drink, as delectable, you mean that it is very pleasant.

복습 sniff [snif] v. 코를 킁킁거리다, 냄새를 맡다
When you sniff, you breathe in air through your nose hard enough to make a sound.

‡‡ hang [hæŋ] v. (hung-hung) 걸다, 달아매다; 매달리다
If something hangs in a high place or position, or if you hang it there, it is attached there so it does not touch the ground.

* embarrassment [imbǽrəsmənt] n. 당황, 곤혹, 난처함
Embarrassment is the feeling you have when you are embarrassed.

9. Wilbur's Boast

* **surrounding** [səráundiŋ] n. 주변(의 상황), 환경, 주위; a. 주위의, 주변의, 부근의
  When you are describing the place where you are at the moment, or the place where you live, you can refer to it as your surroundings.

* **bundle** [bʌ́ndl] n. 묶음, 다발, 꾸러미; vt. 다발[꾸러미]로 하다, 묶다, 싸다
  A bundle of things is a number of them that are tied together or wrapped in a cloth or bag so that they can be carried or stored.

  sweet pea [swi:tpi:] n. 스위트피 (콩과(科)의 원예 식물)
  A sweet pea is a climbing plant which has delicate, sweet-smelling flowers.

* **interrupt** [ìntərʌ́pt] v. 가로막다, 저지하다, 방해하다
  If you interrupt someone who is speaking, you say or do something that causes them to stop.

* **rude** [ru:d] a. 무례한, 버릇없는 (rudely ad. 무례하게)
  When people are rude, they act in an impolite way towards other people or say impolite things about them.

* **twilight** [twáilàit] n. (해뜨기 전·후의) 여명, 황혼, 어스름
  Twilight is the time just before night when the daylight has almost gone but when it is not completely dark.

  whippoorwill [hwípərwìl] n. 쏙독새의 무리
  A whippoorwill is a North American bird that is active at night and has a call that sounds like 'whip poor will'.

* **tobacco** [təbǽkou] n. 담배; 흡연
  Tobacco is dried leaves which people smoke in pipes, cigars, and cigarettes.

* **trill** [tril] n. (새의) 지저귐; 떨리는 목소리; v. 떨리는 소리로 노래하다
  If a bird trills, it sings with short, high-pitched, repeated notes.

  tree toad [tri:toud] n. 청개구리
  A tree toad is any frog that spends a major portion of its lifespan in trees.

* **slam** [slæm] v. (문 따위를) 탕 닫다, 세게 치다; 털썩 내려놓다; n. 쾅 (소리)
  If you slam a door or window or if it slams, it shuts noisily and with great force.

Vocabulary in Charlotte's Web

tremble [trémbəl] v. 떨다, 떨리다
If you tremble, you shake slightly because you are frightened or cold.

thrust [θrʌst] v. 밀치다, 쑤셔 넣다; n. 밀침; 찌름
If you thrust something or someone somewhere, you push or move them there quickly with a lot of force.

whistle [hwísəl] v. 휘파람 불다; n. 휘파람, 호각
When you whistle or when you whistle a tune, you make a series of musical notes by forcing your breath out between your lips, or your teeth.

troupe [tru:p] n. (배우·곡예사 등의) 흥행단, 일당, 한 패
A troupe is a group of actors, singers, or dancers who work together and often travel around together, performing in different places.

piper [páipər] n. 피리 부는 사람
A piper is a musician who plays the bagpipes.

curiosity [kjùəriásəti] n. 호기심; 진기한 것
Curiosity is a desire to know about something.

beg [beg] v. 구걸하다, 빌다; 간절히 바라다
If you beg someone to do something, you ask them very anxiously or eagerly to do it.

slight [slait] a. 근소한, 약간의, 적은; vt. 경시하다; n. 경멸
Something that is slight is very small in degree or quantity.

leave enough idiom 쓸데없는 짓을 하지 않다

nerve [nə:rv] n. 용기, 담력; 신경; 신경과민, 스트레스
Nerve is the courage that you need in order to do something difficult or dangerous.

trough [trɔ(:)f] n. 구유, 여물통
A trough is a long narrow container from which farm animals drink or eat.

mash [mæʃ] vt. 짓찧다, 짓이기다; n. 짓이긴 것
If you mash food that is solid but soft, you crush it so that it forms a soft mass.

9. Wilbur's Boast

delay [diléi] n. 지연; v. 늦추다, 미루다; 우물쭈물하다
A poriod of time when somebody or something has to wait because of a problem that makes something slow or late.

swallow [swálou] ① vt. 들이켜다, 삼키다, 꿀꺽 삼키다 ② n. 제비
To make food, drink, etc. go down your throat into your stomach.

pause [pɔːz] n. 멈춤, 중지; vi. 중단하다, 잠시 멈추다
A pause is a short period when you stop doing something before continuing.

 **Let's walk in the Book**

1. **Which word best described Charlotte before she thought of an idea to save Wilbur?**

    A. Anxious   B. Nervous   C. Patient   D. Unsure

2. **What did Charlotte think of humans?**

    A. She thought that humans were smarter than bugs.
    B. She thought that humans were gullible.
    C. She thought that humans were dangerous.
    D. She thought that humans were untrusting.

10. An Explosion

3. Zuckerman's farm had the best _____ in the county.

   A. blueberry pie   B. place to find large frogs

   C. swing to play on   D. animals

4. Which of the following did the children NOT do together in the afternoon?

   A. They swung on the Zuckerman's swing.

   B. They visited the pigpen.

   C. They built a small tree house.

   D. They ate blueberry pie.

5. Why did Avery try to climb the fence?

   A. He wanted to capture Charlotte.

   B. He wanted to kill Charlotte.

   C. He wanted to break Charlotte's web.

   D. He wanted to make Fern angry.

Vocabulary in Charlotte's Web

motionless [móuʃənlis] a. 움직이지 않는, 부동의, 정지한
Someone or something that is motionless is not moving at all.

patient [péiʃənt] ① a. 인내심[참을성] 있는, 끈기 있는 ② n. 환자, 병자
If you are patient, you stay calm and do not get annoyed.

gullible [gʌ́ləbəl] a. 속기 쉬운, 잘 속는
If you describe someone as gullible, you mean they are easily tricked because they are too trusting.

mercy [mə́ːrsi] n. 행운, 은혜; 자비(심), 인정
If you refer to an event or situation as a mercy, you mean that it makes you feel happy or relieved, usually because it stops something unpleasant happening.

gaze [geiz] vi. 뚫어지게 보다, 응시하다; n. 응시, 주시
If you gaze at someone or something, you look steadily at them for a long time.

affectionate [əfékʃənit] a. 애정이 깊은, 애정 어린
(affectionately ad. 애정을 담고, 애정 어리게)
If you are affectionate, you show your love or fondness for another person in the way that you behave towards them.

wander [wándər] v. (정처 없이) 돌아다니다, 방랑하다
If you wander in a place, you walk around there in a casual way, often without intending to go in any particular direction.

daisy [déizi] n. 데이지
A daisy is a small wild flower with a yellow centre and white petals.

drainboard [dréinbɔːrd] n. (개수대 옆의) 그릇 건조대
The drainboard is the place on a sink unit where things such as cups, plates, and cutlery are put to drain after they have been washed.

scratch [skrætʃ] v. 할퀴다, 긁다; 갈겨쓰다; n. 긁기, 할퀴기
If a sharp object scratches someone or something, it makes small shallow cuts on their skin or surface.

10. An Explosion

dishpan [díʃpæn] n. 설거지통, 개수통
A dishpan is a bowl for washing plates.

soapy [sóupi] a. 비누투성이의, 비누의; 미끄러운
Something that is soapy is full of soap or covered with soap.

★ **henhouse** [hénhàus] n. 닭장, 계사
A henhouse is a special building where hens are kept.

★ **scoop** [sku:p] vt. 퍼 올리다, 푸다, 뜨다; n. 국자, 주걱
If you scoop a person or thing somewhere, you put your hands or arms under or round them and quickly move them there.

복습 **splash** [splæʃ] v. (물·흙탕물 등을) 튀기다; n. 물 튀기기, 첨벙 (물 튀기는 소리)
If you splash water, you hit or disturb the water in a noisy way, causing some of it to fly up into the air.

★ **crisis** [kráisis] n. 위기, 고비; 중대한 기로
A crisis is a situation in which something or someone is affected by one or more very serious problems.

복습 **groan** [groun] v. 신음하다, 끙끙거리다; n. 신음[끙끙거리는] 소리
If you groan, you make a long, low sound because you are in pain, or because you are upset or unhappy about something.

★★ **swing** [swiŋ] v. 흔들다; 매달리다, 빙 돌다; n. 그네; 흔들림
If something swings or if you swing it, it moves repeatedly backwards and forwards or from side to side from a fixed point.

★ **beam** [bi:m] n. 들보, 도리; 광선 v. 빛을 발하다; 밝게 미소 짓다
A beam is a long thick bar of wood, metal, or concrete, especially one used to support the roof of a building.

★★ **bottom** [bátəm] n. 밑(바닥); 기초, 근본; a. 밑바닥의, 최하의, 최저의
The bottom of something is the lowest or deepest part of it.

★ **knot** [nɑt] n. 매듭; 무리, 일파; v. 매다, 매듭을 짓다; 얽히게 하다
If you tie a knot in a piece of string, rope, cloth, or other material, you pass one end or part of it through a loop and pull it tight.

Vocabulary in Charlotte's Web

hayloft [héilɔ̀:ft] n. 건초간, 건초 보관장
hay (n. 건초) + loft (n. 다락)

* **dizzy** [dízi] a. 현기증 나는, 어지러운; 아찔한
If you feel dizzy, you feel as if everything is spinning round and being unable to balance.

straddle [strǽdl] v. 두 발을 벌리다, 두 발로 버티다; n. 두 다리로 버팀
If you straddle something, you put or have one leg on either side of it.

‡ **sail** [seil] v. 항해하다, 출항하다; 뻗어나가다
If a person or thing sails somewhere, they move there smoothly and fairly quickly.

* **zoom** [zu:m] vi. 급상승하다, 붕 소리 내며 질주하다; n. 급상승
If you zoom somewhere, you go there very quickly.

‡ **fear** [fiər] v. 무서워하다, 두려워하다; 걱정하다, 근심하다; n. 무서움, 불안
If you fear someone or something, you are frightened because you think that they will harm you.

‡ **crash** [kræʃ] vt. 충돌하다, 추락하다, 와르르 무너지다; n. 충돌, 추락
If something crashes somewhere, it moves and hits something else violently, making a loud noise.

‡ **tongue** [tʌŋ] n. 혀; 말, 말씨
Your tongue is the soft movable part inside your mouth which you use for tasting, eating, and speaking.

복습 **itch** [itʃ] vi. 가렵다, 근질근질하다; n. 가려움; 안달
When a part of your body itches, you have an unpleasant feeling on your skin that makes you want to scratch.

‡ **pasture** [pǽstʃər] n. 목장, 목초지
Pasture is land with grass growing on it for farm animals to eat.

* **raspberry** [rǽzbèri] n. 나무딸기
Raspberries are small, soft, red fruit that grow on bushes.

94

10. An Explosion

‡ discourage [diskə́:ridʒ] vt. 용기를 잃게 하다, 낙담시키다
If someone or something discourages you, they cause you to lose your enthusiasm about your actions.

‡ suggest [səgdʒést] vt. 제안하다; 암시하다
If you suggest something, you put forward a plan or idea for someone to think about.

‡ capture [kǽptʃər] vt. 붙잡다, 사로잡다; n. 포획
If you capture someone or something, you catch them.

‡ succeed [səksí:d] vi. 성공하다; 잘 되다, 성과를 거두다
If you succeed, you achieve something that you have been aiming for, and if a plan or piece of work succeeds, it has the desired results.

topple [tápəl] vi. 넘어지다, 쓰러지다
If someone or something topples somewhere or if you topple them, they become unsteady or unstable and fall over.

‡ slap [slæp] n. 찰싹 (때림·때리는 소리); v. 찰싹 때리다, 세게 치다
The noise made by hitting somebody or something with the flat part of your hand; A similar noise made by something else.

‡ dull [dʌl] a. 무딘, 둔한; 단조롭고 지루한, 활기 없는
If you describe someone or something as dull, you mean they are not interesting or exciting.

‡ explosion [iksplóuʒən] n. 폭발, 파열
An explosion is a sudden, violent burst of energy, for example one caused by a bomb.

scuttle [skʌ́tl] vi. 급히 가다, 황급히 달리다; 허둥지둥 도망가다; n. 종종걸음
When people or small animals scuttle somewhere, they run there with short quick steps.

복습 stink [stíŋk] n. 악취; v. 고약한 냄새가 나다, 악취가 풍기다, 코를 찌르다
A very unpleasant smell.

‡‡ narrow [nǽrou] a. 간신히 이룬; 폭이 좁은, 한정된
If you have a narrow escape, something unpleasant nearly happens to you.

Vocabulary in Charlotte's Web

- **complaint** [kəmpléint] n. 불평, 불만, 푸념
  A complaint is a statement in which you express your dissatisfaction with a particular situation.

- **share** [ʃɛər] n. 몫, 분담; vt. 분배하다, 공유하다
  The part that somebody has in a particular activity that involves several people.

- **adventure** [ædvéntʃər] n. 모험, 뜻하지 않은 경험; v. 위험을 무릅쓰다
  Adventure is excitement and willingness to do new, unusual, or rather dangerous things.

- **gabble** [gǽbəl] v. 빠르게 지껄이다, 재잘[종알]거리다; n. 허튼 소리
  If you gabble, you say things so quickly that it is difficult for people to understand you.

- **miserable** [mízərəbəl] a. 불쌍한, 비참한, 딱한, 가엾은
  Something that is miserable is very unhappy or uncomfortable.

- **beloved** [bilʌ́vid] a. 가장 사랑하는, 소중한
  A beloved person, thing, or place is one that you feel great affection for.

- **resist** [rizíst] vt. 저항하다, 저지하다
  If you resist something such as a change, you refuse to accept it and try to prevent it.

- **come in handy** idiom 쓸모가 있다, 도움이 되다
  Be useful when needed.

- **unbearable** [ʌnbɛ́ərəbəl] a. 견딜 수 없는, 참을 수 없는
  If you describe something as unbearable, you mean that it is so unpleasant, painful, or upsetting that you feel unable to accept it or deal with it.

- **whisker** [hwískər] n. 수염, 구레나룻
  The whiskers of an animal such as a cat or a mouse are the long stiff hairs that grow near its mouth.

- **pace** [peis] n. 한 발, 걸음; 속도; v. (규칙적으로) 왔다 갔다 하다
  An act of stepping once when walking or running.

10. An Explosion

* **pry** [prai] ① vt. 지레로 들어 올리다, 파내다; n. 지레 ② vi. 엿보다, 동정을 살피다
  If you pry something open or pry it away from a surface, you force it open or away from a surface.

* **bury** [béri] vt. 묻다, 파묻다, 매장하다
  To bury something means to put it into a hole in the ground and cover it up with earth.

* **possession** [pəzéʃən] n. 소유, 입수, 점거, 점령
  If you are in possession of something, you have it, because you have obtained it or because it belongs to you.

  drool [dru:l] vi. 침을 흘리다; n. 허튼 소리, 두서없는 말
  If a person or animal drools, saliva drops slowly from their mouth.

* **pour** [pɔ:r] v. 따르다, 쏟다; vi. 흐르듯이 이동하다, 쇄도하다; 억수같이 퍼붓다
  If you pour a liquid or other substance, you make it flow steadily out of a container by holding the container at an angle.

* **grunt** [grʌnt] vi. (돼지가) 꿀꿀거리다; (사람이) 툴툴거리다; n. 꿀꿀[툴툴]거리는 소리
  When an animal grunts, it makes a low rough noise.

* **gulp** [gʌlp] vt. 꿀꺽꿀꺽 마시다; (긴장·흥분으로) 꿀꺽 삼키다
  If you gulp something, you eat or drink it very quickly by swallowing large quantities of it at once.

  swish [swiʃ] v. 휙 소리를 내다, 휙 움직이다
  If something swishes or if you swish it, it moves quickly through the air, making a soft sound.

  swoosh [swuʃ] v. 휙[쉭] 소리를 내다; 쏴 하고 용솟음치다
  If something swooshes or if you swoosh it, it moves quickly through the air in a way that makes a sound.

* **middling** [mídliŋ] n. (밀기울 섞인) 거친 밀가루; a. 중간치의, 중등의
  A middlings purifier is a device used in the production of flour to remove the husks from the kernels of wheat.

Vocabulary in Charlotte's Web

leftover [léftòuvər] a. 나머지의, 남은; n. 나머지, 찌꺼기
You use leftover to describe an amount of something that remains after the rest of it has been used or eaten.

rind [raind] n. 껍질, 외면, 외견; vt. 껍질을 벗기다, 껍데기를 벗기다
The rind of a fruit such as a lemon or orange is its thick outer skin.

summer squash [sʌ́mərskwɑʃ] n. 호박의 일종
Summer squash are a subset of squashes that are harvested when immature.

stale [steil] a. (음식 따위가) 상한, 신선하지 않은
Stale food is no longer fresh or good to eat.

gingersnap [dʒíndʒərsnæ̀p] n. 생강이 든 쿠키
Gingersnap is a crisp round cookie flavored with ginger.

scum [skʌm] n. 찌끼, 더껑이; v. …에서 뜬 찌꺼기를 걷어내다
Scum is a layer of a dirty or unpleasant-looking substance on the surface of a liquid.

jelly roll [dʒéliroul] n. 젤리 롤, 스위스 롤 (젤리를 바른 스펀지케이크)
Jelly roll is a cylindrical cake made from a thin, flat cake which is covered with jam or cream on one side, then rolled up.

jello [dʒelou] n. 젤로 (과일의 맛과 빛깔과 향을 낸 디저트용 젤리; General Food사의 상표명)
Jello is a cold sweet transparent food made from gelatin, sugar and fruit juice, that shakes when it is moved.

hearty [hɑ́:rti] a. 풍부한; 마음에서 우러난, 원기 왕성한; 건강한
(heartily ad. 진심으로, 마음껏)
(of a meal or somebody's appetite) Large; Making you feel full.

astride [əstráid] a. 걸터앉아, 올라타고, 두 다리를 쩍 벌리고
If you sit or stand astride something, you sit or stand with one leg on each side of it.

moody [mú:di] a. 침울한, 언짢은; 변덕스러운 (moodily ad. 침울하게)
If you describe something as moody, you mean that it suggests particular emotions, especially sad ones.

10. An Explosion

bestir [bistə́:r] vt. 꾸물대지 않고 움직이다, 부지런히 일하다; 분발하다
If you bestir, you start doing things after a period during which you have been doing nothing.

descend [disénd] v. 내려가다, 내리다
If you descend or if you descend a staircase, you move downwards from a higher to a lower level.

drowse [drauz] v. 꾸벅꾸벅 졸다; 멍하니 있다; n. 겉잠, 졸음
If you drowse, you are almost asleep or just asleep.

snooze [snu:z] v. 꾸벅꾸벅 졸다; n. 선잠, 앉아 졸기
If you snooze, you sleep lightly for a short period of time.

thread [θred] n. 실, 바느질 실; vt. 실을 꿰다
Thread or a thread is a long very thin piece of a material such as cotton, nylon, or silk.

Let's walk in the Book

1. **Why was Charlotte's web easy to see in the morning?**
   A. It rained the night before and the web was wet.
   B. The sunlight in the morning made the web shine.
   C. Charlotte's web so large that it covered most of the barn door.
   D. It was a foggy morning and the web was covered with beads of water.

2. **Which of the following was NOT true when Lurvy saw the web?**
   A. Lurvy went on his knees and said a short prayer.
   B. Lurvy fed Wilbur and walked back to the farm house.
   C. Lurvy brushed his hands across his eyes.
   D. Lurvy thought that he was seeing things.

3. **How did Mr. Zuckerman look when he told his wife about the web?**
   A. She looked pale and frightened.
   B. She looked confident and amazed.
   C. She looked confused.
   D. She looked excited and curious.

11. The Miracle

4. What did Mrs. Zuckerman believe was NOT ordinary about the farm?

A. She believed that Wilbur was not an ordinary pig.
B. She believed that all the animals on the farm were not ordinary animals.
C. She believed that Charlotte was not an ordinary spider.
D. She believed that Mr. Zuckerman was not an ordinary man.

5. Why did Wilbur enjoy the Zuckermans and Lurvy around his pen?

A. He liked that Charlotte's web was getting so much attention.
B. He thought that he would get more food.
C. He enjoyed the attention he was getting.
D. He thought that they would give him a special treat.

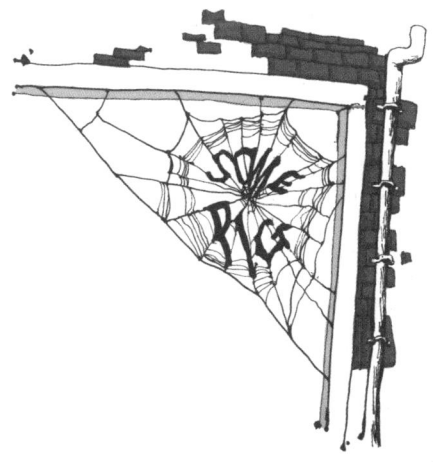

Vocabulary in Charlotte's Web

* **foggy** [fɔ́(ː)gi] a. 안개가 자욱한; 침침한, 흐린; (생각 등이) 몽롱한; 막연한
  When it is foggy, there is fog.

* **drip** [drip] v. 물방울이 떨어지다; n. 똑똑 떨어지기
  When liquid drips somewhere, or you drip it somewhere, it falls in individual small drops.

* **asparagus** [əspǽrəgəs] n. 아스파라거스
  Asparagus is a vegetable that is long and green and has small shoots at one end.

* **patch** [pætʃ] n. (채소나 과일을 기르는) 작은 땅; 헝겊 조각; v. 헝겊을 대고 깁다; 수선하다
  A patch of land is a small area of land where a particular plant or crop grows.

* **strand** [strænd] ① n. 가닥, 외가닥으로 꼰 끈 ② v. 좌초시키다; 오도 가도 못하다
  A strand of something such as hair, wire, or thread is a single thin piece of it.

* **dozen** [dʌ́zn] n. 상당히 많음; 1다스, 12개; a. 1다스의, 12(개)의
  If you refer to dozens of things or people, you are emphasizing that there are very many of them.

* **bead** [biːd] n. 구슬, 유리알; 방울; vt. 구슬로 장식하다
  Beads are small pieces of colored glass, wood, or plastic with a hole through the middle.

* **glisten** [glísn] vi. 반짝이다, 빛나다
  If something glistens, it shines, usually because it is wet or oily.

* **delicate** [délikət] a. 섬세한, 고운; 우아한; 예민한; 미묘한
  Something that is delicate is small and beautifully shaped.

* **veil** [veil] n. 베일, 면사포, 덮개; v. 덮다, 숨기다, 감추다
  A veil is a piece of thin soft cloth that women sometimes wear over their heads and which can also cover their face.

* **neat** [niːt] a. 산뜻한, 깔끔한 (neatly ad. 깔끔하게)
  A neat place, thing, or person is tidy and smart, and has everything in the correct place.

11. The Miracle

whisper [hwíspər] v. 속삭이다, 작은 목소리로 말하다; n. 속삭임
When you whisper, you say something very quietly, using your breath rather than your throat.

utter [ʌ́tər] ① v. 입 밖에 내다; 발언하다 ② a. 완전한, 전적인, 절대적인
If someone utters sounds or words, they say them.

murmur [mə́:rmər] v. 속삭이다, 낮은 목소리로 말하다; n. 사각사각하는 소리; 중얼거림
If you murmur something, you say it very quietly, so that not many people can hear what you are saying.

exertion [igzə́:rʃən] n. 노력, 분발
Extertion is the physical or mental effort or the act of making an effort.

mutter [mʌ́tər] v. 중얼거리다, 불평하다; n. 중얼거림, 불평
If you mutter, you speak very quietly so that you cannot easily be heard, often because you are complaining about something.

solemn [sáləm] a. 엄숙한, 근엄한 (solemnly ad. 장엄하게, 진지하게)
Someone or something that is solemn is very serious rather than cheerful or humorous.

unusual [ʌnjú:ʒuəl] a. 보통이 아닌, 비범한; 별난, 유다른
Usual is used to describe what happens or what is done most often in a particular situation.

bewilder [biwíldər] vt. 당황하게[어리둥절하게] 하다 (bewilderment n. 당황, 어리둥절함)
To confuse somebody.

ordinary [ɔ́:rdənèri] a. 보통의, 평범한
Ordinary people or things are normal and not special or different in any way.

distinct [distíŋkt] a. 뚜렷한, 분명한; 별개의
If something is distinct, you can hear, see, or taste it clearly.

spang [spæŋ] ad. 완전히, 정확히, 정통으로
Spang means directly.

occur [əkə́:r] vi. 일어나다, 생기다; 생각이 떠오르다
When something occurs, it happens.

Vocabulary in Charlotte's Web

blunder [blʌ́ndər] v. 걸려서 넘어질 뻔하다; 큰 실수를 하다, 일을 그르치다; n. 큰 실수
If you blunder somewhere, you move there in a clumsy and careless way.

extra [ékstrə] a. 특별한; 여분의, 임시의; n. 할증 요금; 번외
You use extra to describe an amount, person, or thing that is added to others of the same kind, or that can be added to others of the same kind.

solid [sálid] a. 최고인, 멋진; 고체의; 견실[견고]한; n. 고체
If you describe someone as solid, you mean that they are very reliable and respectable.

minister [mínistər] n. 성직자, 목사; 장관, 대신, 각료
A minister is a member of the clergy, especially in Protestant churches.

sermon [sə́:rmən] n. 설교; 잔소리
A sermon is a talk on a religious or moral subject that is given by a member of the clergy as part of a church service.

wondrous [wʌ́ndrəs] a. 놀랄 만한, 불가사의한
If you describe something as wondrous, you mean it is strange and beautiful or impressive.

niece [niːs] n. 조카딸, 질녀
Someone's niece is the daughter of their sister or brother.

queer [kwiər] a. 언짢은; 별난, 기묘한; 수상한
Something that is queer is strange.

notion [nóuʃən] n. 생각, 개념, 관념
A notion is an idea or belief about something.

spread [spred] v. 펴다, 펼치다, 뿌리다; n. 퍼짐, 폭
If you spread something somewhere, you open it out or arrange it over a place or surface, so that all of it can be seen or used easily.

gyromatic transmission n. 반자동 변속기 (Dodge사에서 명명)

rattle [rǽtl] v. 덜거덕거리며 움직이다; n. 덜거덕거리는 소리
When something rattles or when you rattle it, it makes short sharp knocking sounds because it is being shaken or it keeps hitting against something hard.

11. The Miracle

* **buggy** [bʌ́gi] ① n. 자동차, 마차 ② a. 벌레투성이의; 미친, 열중하고 있는
  A buggy is a small lightweight carriage pulled by one horse.

  buckboard [bʌ́kbɔ̀ːrd] n. (차체가 판자로 된) 4륜 짐마차
  A buckboard is a four-wheeled wagon of simple construction meant to be drawn by a horse or other large animal.

* **miraculous** [mirǽkjələs] a. 기적적인, 초자연적인; 놀랄 만한
  If you describe a good event as miraculous, you mean that it is very surprising and unexpected.

‡ **punish** [pʌ́niʃ] vt. 벌하다, 응징하다, 처벌하다 (punishment n. 벌, 징벌)
  To punish someone means to make them suffer in some way because they have done something wrong.

‡ **prepare** [pripɛ́ər] v. 준비하다, 채비하다
  If you prepare something, you make it ready for something that is going to happen.

‡ **shave** [ʃeiv] v. (수염 등을) 깎다, 면도하다; n. 면도 (도구)
  When a man shaves, he removes the hair from his face using a razor or shaver so that his face is smooth.

‡ **principal** [prínsəpəl] a. 주요한, 주된; 중요한; n. 우두머리, 장
  Principal means first in order of importance.

‡ **ripe** [raip] a. 익은, 여문
  Ripe fruit or grain is fully grown and ready to eat.

* **hoe** [hou] v. (잡초를) 파내다; 괭이질하다; n. (자루가 긴) 괭이
  To break up soil, remove plants, etc. with a hoe.

‡ **prove** [pruːv] v. …임이 알려지다; 입증[증명]하다; 시험하다
  If something proves to be true, it becomes clear after a period of time that it is true.

  all in all idiom 종합해서 말하면, 대체로[대강] 말하면
  All in all is used to introduce a statement, when everything is considered.

‡ **attraction** [ətrǽkʃən] n. 인기거리; 매력, 유혹; 끌어당김, 흡인
  An attraction is a feature which makes something interesting or desirable.

 Let's walk in the Book

1. **Who was not present at the beginning of the meeting?**
   A. Gander
   B. Templeton
   C. The oldest sheep
   D. The lambs

2. **Why didn't Charlotte like the suggestion, 'Pig Supreme?'**
   A. She thought it would be too difficult to write in the web.
   B. She thought it sounded egotistical.
   C. She thought it sounded like a dessert.
   D. She thought that the people wouldn't like it.

12. A Meeting

3. Who did Charlotte think the word Terrific would impress the most?

A. The minister
B. Fern
C. The townspeople
D. Mr. Zuckerman

4. The animals thought that _____ could give them more ideas for the web.

A. Fern and her books
B. Templeton
C. old newspapers
D. old magazines

5. Why did Charlotte doubt that Templeton would help?

A. She thought Templeton was too selfish.
B. She thought that Templeton was too lazy to go to the dump.
C. She thought that Templeton wouldn't know what she needed from the dump.
D. She thought that Templeton didn't like her.

Vocabulary in Charlotte's Web

cellar [sélər] n. 지하실, 지하층
A cellar is a room underneath a building, which is often used for storing things in.

call the roll phrasal v. 출석을 부르다
If you call the roll, you check which of the members of a group are present by reading their names out.

idiosyncrasy [ìdiəsíŋkrəsi] n. (개인의) 특질, 특징, 개성
If you talk about the idiosyncrasies of someone or something, you are referring to their rather unusual habits or characteristics.

glare [glɛər] v. 노려보다; 번쩍번쩍 빛나다; n. 섬광; 노려봄
If you glare at someone, you look at them with an angry expression on your face.

proceed [prousí:d] vi. 속행하다, 계속하다; 나아가다, 가다
If an activity, process, or event proceeds, it goes on and does not stop.

praise [preiz] vt. 칭찬하다; n. 칭찬, 찬양
To express your approval or admiration for somebody or something.

dare [dɛər] v. 감히 …하다, 무릅쓰다, 도전하다; n. 도전; 용기
If you dare to do something, you do something which requires a lot of courage.

hurray [huréi] n. 만세 소리, 환호성; v. 만세를 부르다, 환호하다
People sometimes shout 'Hurray!' when they are very happy and excited about something.

remark [rimá:rk] n. 의견, 말; 주의; v. …에 주의[주목]하다; 말하다
If you make a remark about something, you say something about it.

slogan [slóugən] n. 슬로건, 모토, 표어; 함성
A slogan is a short phrase that is easy to remember.

supreme [səprí:m] a. 최고의, 최상의; n. 최고의 것
You use supreme to emphasize that a quality or thing is very great.

12. A Meeting

* **terrific** [tərífik] a. 굉장한, 빼어난; 무서운
  If you describe something or someone as terrific, you are very pleased with them or very impressed by them.

* **impress** [imprés] vt. …에게 감명을 주다, 감동시키다
  If something impresses you, you feel great admiration for it.

  acrobat [ǽkrəbæt] n. 곡예사
  An acrobat is an entertainer who performs difficult physical acts such as jumping and balancing, especially in a circus.

* **tear** [tɛər] ① v. (tore-torn) 째지다, 찢어지다 ② n. 눈물
  If you tear paper, cloth, or another material, or if it tears, you pull it into two pieces or you pull it so that a hole appears in it.

* **advertisement** [ædvərtáizmənt] n. 광고, 선전
  An advertisement is an announcement in a newspaper, on television, or on a poster about something such as a product, event, or job.

* **fellow** [félou] n. 친구, 동료; 사나이, 녀석
  You use fellow to describe people who are in the same situation as you, or people you feel you have something in common with.

* **appeal** [əpíːl] vi. 마음에 호소하다; 애원하다, 간청하다; n. 애원, 간청
  If you appeal to someone to do something, you make a serious and urgent request to them.

* **instinct** [ínstiŋkt] n. 본능, 직관, 천성
  Instinct is the natural tendency that a person or animal has to behave or react in a particular way.

* **plenty** [plénti] n. 많음, 풍부; 충분
  Plenty is used especially to indicate that there is enough of something, or more than you need.

* **creep** [kriːp] vi. 기다, 살금살금 걷다; n. 포복
  When people or animals creep somewhere, they move quietly and slowly.

Vocabulary in Charlotte's Web

- **assemble** [əsémbəl] v. 모으다, 모이다; 조립하다
  When people assemble or when someone assembles them, they come together in a group, usually for a particular purpose such as a meeting.

- **bore** [bɔːr] v. 지루하게[따분하게] 하다; n. 따분한[하기 싫은] 것
  If someone or something bores you, you find them dull and uninteresting.

- **clipping** [klípiŋ] n. (신문·잡지의) 오려낸 기사; 가위질, 깎기
  A clipping is an article, picture, or advertisement that has been cut from a newspaper or magazine.

- **pail** [peil] n. 들통, 버킷
  A pail is a bucket, usually made of metal or wood.

- **slop** [slɑp] n. (돼지 사료용) 밥찌꺼기; 엎지름, 흙탕물; v. 엎지르다, 엎질러서 더럽히다
  You can use slop or slops to refer to liquid waste containing the remains of food.

- **chief** [tʃiːf] a. 주요한; 최고의, 제1위의; n. 장, 우두머리, 지배자
  The chief cause, part, or member of something is the most important one.

- **destiny** [déstəni] n. 운명, 숙명; 하늘(의 뜻)
  What happens to somebody or what will happen to them in the future, especially things that they cannot change or avoid.

- **whisker** [hwískər] n. 수염, 구레나룻
  The whiskers of an animal such as a cat or a mouse are the long stiff hairs that grow near its mouth.

- **quiver** [kwívər] vi. 떨리다, 흔들리다
  If something quivers, it shakes with very small movements.

- **gruff** [grʌf] a. (목소리가) 거친, 쉰; 퉁명스러운 (gruffly ad. 거칠게; 퉁명스럽게)
  A gruff voice sounds low and rough.

- **adjourn** [ədʒə́ːrn] v. 휴회[폐회]하다, 연기하다
  If a meeting or trial is adjourned or if it adjourns, it is stopped for a short time.

12. A Meeting

‡ average [ǽvəridʒ] a. 평균의, 보통 수준의; n. 평균; 표준, 보통 수준
An average person or thing is typical or normal.

‡ concern [kənsə́:rn] vt. …에 관계하다; 걱정시키다, 걱정하다; n. 관계; 관심
If you concern yourself with something, you give it attention because you think that it is important.

‡ sensational [senséiʃənəl] a. 선풍적 인기의, 세상을 깜짝 놀라게 하는; 지각의
A sensational result, event, or situation is so remarkable that it causes great excitement and interest.

Let's walk in the Book

1. **Why did Charlotte decide to use dry thread to make the letters?**
   A. She didn't want the letters to get wet.
   B. She didn't want the letters to get dirty.
   C. She didn't want bugs to get stuck to the letters.
   D. She wanted it to be thicker and easier to see.

2. **Mr. Zuckerman wanted _____ to hear about his terrific pig.**
   A. the town mayor
   B. all of his friends
   C. the president
   D. the local paper

3. **Where would Mr. Zuckerman take Wilbur in September?**
   A. He would take Wilbur to the County Fair.
   B. He would take Wilbur to the zoo.
   C. He would take Wilbur to make an appearance on the local news.
   D. He would take Wilbur to a butcher.

4. **Charlotte didn't like the word crunchy because _____**
   A. she thought it was an ugly word.
   B. she thought it would remind Mr. Zuckerman of bacon and ham.
   C. she thought Templeton was being rude towards Wilbur.
   D. she thought it would be too difficult to write in the web.

13. Good Progress

5. From which item did Charlotte find the new word for the web?

A. A label from a shirt

B. An advertisement from a magazine

C. A piece from a soap package

D. A piece from a cereal box

Vocabulary in Charlotte's Web

- **rip** [rip] vt. 쪼개다, 째다, 찢다, 벗겨내다
  When something rips or when you rip it, you tear it forcefully.

- **orb** [ɔːrb] n. 구, 원; vt. 공 모양으로 만들다, 둥글게 하다
  An orb is something that is shaped like a ball, for example the sun or moon.

- **radial** [réidiəl] a. 반지름의; 광선의
  Radial refers to the pattern that you get when straight lines are drawn from the centre of a circle to a number of points round the edge.

- **produce** [prədjúːs] v. 만들어 내다; 생산하다, 제조하다; n. 생산액
  If you produce something, you make or create it.

- **foundation** [faundéiʃən] n. 기초, 토대; 설립, 재단
  The foundation of something such as a belief or way of life is the things on which it is based.

- **sticky** [stíki] a. 끈적[끈끈]한, 들러붙는
  A sticky substance is soft, or thick and liquid, and can stick to other things.

- **snare** [snɛər] n. 덫, 올가미, 유혹; vt. 덫으로 잡다, 유혹하다
  A snare is a trap for catching birds or small animals. It consists of a loop of wire or rope which pulls tight around the animal.

- **tube** [tjuːb] n. 관 모양의 기관; 관, 통; vt. …에 관을 달다, 관 속에 넣다
  Some long, thin, hollow parts in your body are referred to as tubes.

- **descend** [disénd] v. 내려가다, 내리다
  If you descend or if you descend a staircase, you move downwards from a higher to a lower level.

- **ascend** [əsénd] v. 올라가다, 오르다
  If something ascends, it moves up.

- **task** [tæsk] n. 힘든 일, 노역; 직무, 과제, 과업
  A task is an activity or piece of work which you have to do, usually as part of a larger project.

- **beneath** [biníːθ] prep. …의 아래[밑]에, …보다 낮게; …할 가치가 없는
  Something that is beneath another thing is under the other thing.

13. Good Progress

* **lung** [lʌŋ] n. 폐, 허파
  Your lungs are the two organs inside your chest which fill with air when you breathe in.

* **dew** [dju:] n. 이슬; 신선함, 상쾌함; v. 이슬로 적시다; 축이다, 눅눅하게 하다
  Dew is small drops of water that form on the ground and other surfaces outdoors during the night.

* **swell** [swel] v. 부풀다, 팽창하다; 증가시키다, 복받쳐 오르다
  If something such as a part of your body swells, it becomes larger and rounder than normal.

* **snout** [snaut] n. (돼지 등의) 코, 주둥이
  The snout of an animal such as a pig is its long nose.

* **chest** [tʃest] ① n. 가슴 ② n. 상자, 궤
  Your chest is the top part of the front of your body where your ribs, lungs, and heart are.

* **chronicle** [kránikl] n. …신문; 연대기, 이야기, 기록
  Chronicle is sometimes used as part of the name of a newspaper.

* **journey** [dʒə́ːrni] vi. 여행하다; n. 여행
  If you journey somewhere, you travel there.

* **tie-up** [táiʌp] n. (미) 소 외양간; 정체; 불통, 휴업, 협력, 제휴
  A farm building in which cows are kept.

* **furthermore** [fə́ːrðərmɔ̀ːr] ad. 더욱이, 게다가, 더군다나
  In addition; More importantly.

* **crate** [kreit] n. 나무 상자
  A crate is a large box used for transporting or storing things.

* **pitch fork** [pítʃfɔ̀ːrk] n. 건초용 포크, (세 가닥) 갈퀴
  A pitch fork is an agricultural tool with a long handle and long, thin, widely separated pointed tines used to lift and pitch.

* **below** [bilóu] prep. …보다 아래[밑]에; ad. 아래로[에]; a. 하단의, 후술의
  If something is below something else, it is in a lower position.

Vocabulary in Charlotte's Web

orchard [ɔ́:rtʃərd] n. 과수원
An orchard is an area of land on which fruit trees are grown.

alder [ɔ́:ldər] n. 오리나무
An alder is a species of tree or shrub that grows especially in cool, damp places and loses its leaves in winter.

astonish [əstániʃ] vt. 깜짝 놀라게 하다 (astonishing a. 놀라운)
If something or someone astonishes you, they surprise you very much.

tin [tin] n. 주석, 양철; 깡통, 냄비
Tin is a soft silvery-white metal.

rag [ræg] n. 넝마, 걸레
A rag is a piece of old cloth which you can use to clean or wipe things.

hinge [hindʒ] n. 경첩, 돌쩌귀
A hinge is a piece of metal, wood, or plastic that is used to join a door to its frame or to join two things together so that one of them can swing freely.

discard [diská:rd] vt. 버리다, 처분하다; n. 버림(받음)
If you discard something, you get rid of it because you no longer want it or need it.

dishmop [díʃmap] n. 그릇 씻는 수세미
dish (n. 그릇) + mop (n. 걸레, 자루걸레)

tatter [tǽtər] v. 갈가리 찢대[찢어지다]; n. 넝마, 누더기 옷
If something such as clothing or a book is tattered, it is damaged or torn.

overall [óuvərɔ̀:l] n. 멜빵과 가슴받이가 달린 작업복; a. 전부의, 전체에 걸친
Overalls are trousers that are attached to a piece of cloth which covers your chest and which has straps going over your shoulders.

rust [rʌst] n. (금속의) 녹; v. 녹슬다, 부식하다 (rusty a. 녹슨)
Rust is a brown substance that forms on iron or steel, when it comes into contact with water.

13. Good Progress

spike [spaik] n. 대못, 담장 못; vt. 큰 못으로 박다; 못[말뚝]을 박다
A narrow thin shape with a sharp point at one end, or something, especially a piece of metal, with this shape.

leaky [líːki] a. 새는, 새기 쉬운
Something that is leaky has holes, cracks, or other faults which allow liquids and gases to pass through.

stopper [stápər] n. (병·통 따위의) 마개, 꼭지; 멈추는 사람[물건], 방해자
A stopper is a piece of glass, plastic, or cork that fits into the top of a bottle or jar to close it.

* **crank** [kræŋk] n. 크랭크, ㄴ자형 손잡이; v. 크랭크로 움직이다
To make something move by turning a crank. A crank is a device that you turn in order to make something move.

* **freezer** [fríːzər] n. 냉동 장치, 냉동실; 아이스크림 제조기
A freezer is a large container like a fridge in which the temperature is kept below freezing point so that you can store food inside it for long periods.

* **cling** [kliŋ] vi. 달라붙다, 매달리다
If you cling to someone or something, you hold onto them tightly.

rummage [rʌ́midʒ] v. 뒤지다, 샅샅이 찾다
If you rummage through something, you search for something you want by moving things around in a careless or hurried way.

crunchy [krʌ́ntʃi] a. 우두둑 깨무는[소리 나는]; 자박자박 밟는
Food that is crunchy is pleasantly hard or crisp so that it makes a noise when you eat it.

* **crisp** [krisp] a. 파삭파삭한, 아삭아삭하는; 상쾌한; n. 파삭파삭한 것
Food that is crisp is pleasantly hard, or has a pleasantly hard surface.

* **noble** [nóubəl] a. 고귀한, 고결한; 귀족의
If you describe something as noble, you think that its appearance or quality is very impressive, making it superior to other things of its type.

Vocabulary in Charlotte's Web

label [léibəl] n. 라벨, 꼬리표; vt. 라벨을[표를] 붙이다
A piece of paper or other material which gives you information about the object it is fixed to.

preshrunk [priːʃrʌ́ŋk] a. 방축 가공한
Preshrunk fabric is that fabric may shrink up.

shrink [ʃriŋk] v. (shrunk-shrunk(en)) 오그라들다, 줄다; 축소시키다, 움츠리게 하다
If something shrinks or something else shrinks it, it becomes smaller.

grumble [grʌ́mbəl] v. 불평하다, 툴툴대다; n. 투덜댐
If someone grumbles, they complain about something in a bad-tempered way.

woodshed [wúdʃèd] n. 목재 헛간 (wood 나무, 목재 + shed 오두막, 우리)
A woodshed is a small building which is used for storing wood for a fire.

ceiling [síːliŋ] n. 천장; 최고 한도
A ceiling is the horizontal surface that forms the top part or roof inside a room.

triumphant [traiʌ́mfənt] a. 승리를 한, 의기양양한 (triumphantly ad. 의기양양하게)
Someone who is triumphant has gained a victory or succeeded in something and feels very happy about it.

radiant [réidiənt] a. 빛나는, 밝은
Something that is radiant glows brightly.

flake [fleik] n. 조각, 파편; 한 조각; v. 조각으로 벗겨지다[떼어내다]
A small, very thin layer or piece of something, especially one that has broken off from sth larger.

fetch [fetʃ] vt. 가져오다, 데려오다, 불러오다
If you fetch something or someone, you go and get them from the place where they are.

gallop [gǽləp] vi. 전속력으로 달리다, 질주하다; n. 갤럽[전속력]
If you gallop, you run somewhere very quickly.

13. Good Progress

- **flip** [flip] n. 공중제비; 가볍게 침; v. (손가락으로) 튀기다, 홱 뒤집다
  A movement in which the body turns over in the air.

- **writhe** [raið] v. 몸부림치다, 몸을 비틀다; n. 몸부림, 뒹굴기; 고뇌
  To twist or move your body without stopping, often because you are in great pain.

- **romp** [rɑmp] n. 떠들며 뛰어놀기, 활발한 장난; v. 떠들썩하게 뛰놀다
  When children or animals romp, they play noisily and happily.

- **scratch** [skrætʃ] v. 할퀴다, 긁다; 갈겨쓰다; n. 긁기, 할퀴기
  (scratchy a. 가려운, 따끔따끔한)
  If a sharp object scratches someone or something, it makes small shallow cuts on their skin or surface.

- **cousin** [kʌ́zn] n. 사촌, 종형제; 친척
  Your cousin is the child of your uncle or aunt.

- **stream** [striːm] n. 시내, 개울; 흐름; v. 흐르다
  A stream is a small narrow river.

- **leap** [liːp] v. 껑충 뛰다, 도약하다; 뛰어넘다; n. 뜀, 도약; 급변
  If you leap, you jump high in the air or jump a long distance.

- **tangle** [tǽŋgəl] v. 얽히게 하다; 엉키다; n. 엉킴; 혼란
  If something is tangled or tangles, it becomes twisted together in an untidy way.

- **thrash** [θræʃ] v. 뒹굴다, 몸부림치다; 마구 때리다
  If someone thrashes about, or thrashes their arms or legs about, they move in a wild or violent way.

- **tackle** [tǽkəl] v. 달려들다; 부딪치다; n. 연장, 도구; 태클
  If you tackle someone, you attack them and fight them.

- **swoop** [swuːp] v. 내리 덮치다, 달려들다; 급강하하다
  When a bird or airplane swoops, it suddenly moves downwards through the air in a smooth curving movement.

Vocabulary in Charlotte's Web

* **fin** [fin] n. 지느러미
A fish's fins are the flat objects which stick out of its body and help it to swim and keep its balance.

sag [sæg] v. 처지다, 축 늘어지다; 나른해지다
When something sags, it hangs down loosely or sinks downwards in the middle.

복습 **dodge** [dɑdʒ] v. 휙 피하다, 날쌔게 비키다
If you dodge, you move suddenly, often to avoid being hit, caught, or seen.

* **merciless** [mɔ́ːrsilis] a. 무자비한, 무정한, 잔인한 (mercilessly ad. 무자비하게, 잔인하게)
Showing no kindness or pity.

복습 **lash** [læʃ] ① v. 심하게 움직이다; 세차게 부딪히다 ② n. (= eyelash) 속눈썹
If an animal lashes its tail, or if its tail lashes, it moves its tail very fast and violently.

복습 **budge** [bʌdʒ] v. 움직이기 시작하다; 태도[견해]를 바꾸다
If someone or something will not budge, they will not move.

aeronaut [ɛ́ərənɔ̀ːt] n. 기구[비행선] 조종사
An aeronaut is the pilot of a lighter-than-air aircraft, especially a balloon.

balloonist [bəlúːnist] n. (스포츠·취미로) 기구 타는 사람
A balloonist is a person who flies a hot-air balloon.

* **lullaby** [lʌ́ləbài] n. 자장가
A lullaby is a quiet song which is intended to be sung to babies and young children to help them go to sleep.

복습 **cricket** [kríkit] n. 귀뚜라미
A cricket is a small jumping insect that produces short, loud sounds by rubbing its wings together.

* **chirp** [tʃəːrp] v. 짹짹 울다; (즐거운 듯이) 말하다; n. 짹짹 (새 등의 울음소리)
When a bird or an insect such as a cricket or grasshopper chirps, it makes short high-pitched sounds.

13. Good Progress

dung [dʌŋ] n. 거름, 비료; 똥; vt. 비료를 주다
Dung is faeces from animals, especially from large animals such as cattle and horses.

* **thrush** [θrʌʃ] n. 개똥지빠귀
A thrush is a fairly small bird with a brown back and a spotted breast.

 **Let's walk in the Book**

1. **Fern's mother believed that Fern made up _____**
   A. Wilbur's stories.
   B. stories about the farm.
   C. Charlotte's stories.
   D. stories she heard from her playmates.

2. **Fern's mother thought that Fern being in the barn cellar was a bad idea because _____**
   A. she thought it was too dangerous being there alone.
   B. she thought Fern wasn't spending enough time at home.
   C. she thought Fern wasn't spending enough time with her family.
   D. she thought Fern was spending too much time alone.

3. **Why did Mrs. Arable go to Dr. Dorian's office?**
   A. She was worried about Fern's physical health.
   B. She was worried about the plots of Fern's stories.
   C. She thought it was unnatural for Fern to be so interested in animals.
   D. She thought that Fern must be very sick if Fern heard animals talk.

14. Dr. Dorian

4. What did Dr. Dorian think was a miracle that nobody noticed?

   A. The writing in Charlotte's web

   B. The making of a spider's web

   C. Wilbur

   D. Fern hearing animals talk

5. Why did Mrs. Arable not like the words in the web?

   A. She didn't think there was anything special about the web.

   B. She thought the words were a hoax.

   C. She didn't like things she couldn't understand.

   D. She thought the spider could be dangerous.

Vocabulary in Charlotte's Web

storyteller [stɔ́:ritèlər] n. 이야기 잘하는 사람; 소설 작가; 민담[야담]가
A storyteller is someone who tells or writes stories.

poke [pouk] v. 찌르다, 쑤시다, 들이대다; n. 찌름, 쑤심
If you poke someone or something, you quickly push them with your finger or with a sharp object.

bowl [boul] n. 사발, 공기, 주발
A bowl is a round container with a wide uncovered top.

stern [stɔ́:rn] a. 엄한, 단호한 (sternly ad. 엄하게, 단호하게)
Stern words or actions are very severe.

invent [invént] vt. 날조하다, 조작하다; 발명하다, 고안하다
If you invent a story or excuse, you try to make other people believe that it is true when in fact it is not.

fascinate [fǽsənèit] v. 매혹하다, 반하게 하다; 마음을 빼앗다
If something fascinates you, it interests and delights you so much that your thoughts tend to concentrate on it.

fib [fib] vi. 악의 없는 거짓말을 하다; n. 사소한[악의 없는] 거짓말
If someone is fibbing, they are telling lies.

snap [snæp] v. 날카롭게[느닷없이] 말하다; 홱 잡다, 짤깍 소리 내다; n. 툭 소리냄
If someone snaps at you, they speak to you in a sharp, unfriendly way.

curiosity [kjùəriásəti] n. 호기심; 진기한 것
Curiosity is a desire to know about something.

vague [veig] a. 어렴풋한, 막연한 (vaguely ad. 모호하게, 막연하게)
If something written or spoken is vague, it does not explain or express things clearly.

aloft [əlɔ́(:)ft] ad. 위에, 높이, 공중에
Something that is aloft is in the air or off the ground.

playmate [pléimèit] n. 놀이 친구
A child's playmate is another child who often plays with him or her.

14. Dr. Dorian

* **sociable** [sóuʃəbəl] a. 사교적인; 붙임성 있는
  Sociable people are friendly and enjoy talking to other people.

* **dust** [dʌst] v. 먼지를 떨다, 청소하다; n. 먼지, 티끌
  When you dust something such as furniture, you remove dust from it, usually using a cloth.

* **advice** [ədváis] n. 충고, 조언, 권고
  If you give someone advice, you tell them what you think they should do in a particular situation.

* **beard** [biərd] n. 턱수염
  A man's beard is the hair that grows on his chin and cheeks.

* **enchant** [entʃǽnt] vt. 매혹하다, 황홀케 하다
  If you are enchanted by someone or something, they cause you to have feelings of great delight or pleasure.

* **shift** [ʃift] v. 방향을 바꾸다, 옮기다; n. 교대, 순환; 변화, 이동
  If you shift something or if it shifts, it moves slightly.

  crochet [krouʃéi] v. 코바늘로 뜨개질하다; v. 코바늘 뜨개질
  If you crochet, you make cloth by using a needle with a small hook at the end.

  doily [dɔ́ili] n. (레이스 등으로 만든) 탁상용 작은 그릇을 받치는 깔개
  A doily is a small, round piece of paper or cloth that has a pattern of tiny holes in it.

* **instruction** [instrʌ́kʃən] n. 지령, 지시; 가르침, 교훈
  An instruction is something that someone tells you to do.

* **regard** [rigá:rd] vt. 간주하다, …으로 여기다; n. 주목, 주의; 안부
  If you regard someone or something as being a particular thing or as having a particular quality, you believe that they are that thing or have that quality.

* **sigh** [sai] v. 한숨 쉬다; n. 한숨, 탄식
  When you sigh, you let out a deep breath, as a way of expressing feelings such as disappointment, tiredness, or pleasure.

Vocabulary in Charlotte's Web

fidget [fídʒit] v. 안절부절 못하다, 불안해하다
If you fidget, you keep moving your hands or feet slightly or changing your position slightly, for example because you are nervous, bored, or excited.

civil [sívəl] a. 예의 바른, 정중한; 시민의, 문명의 (civilly ad. 예의바르게, 정중하게)
Someone who is civil is polite in a formal way, but not particularly friendly.

grownup [gróunʌ̀p] n. 어른, 성인; a. 성숙한, 어른이 된, 어른다운
(used by or to children) A grownup is an adult.

incessant [insésənt] a. 끊임없는, 그칠 새 없는, 쉴 새 없는
An incessant process or activity is one that continues without stopping.

appetite [ǽpitàit] n. 식욕, 욕구
Your appetite is your desire to eat.

doubt [daut] v. 의심하다, 수상히 여기다; n. 의심, 회의; 불신
If you are in doubt about something, you feel unsure or uncertain about it.

mumble [mʌ́mbəl] v. 중얼[웅얼]거리다; 우물우물 씹다; n. 중얼거림
If you mumble, you speak very quietly and not at all clearly with the result that the words are difficult to understand.

remarkable [rimá:rkəbəl] a. 비범한, 뛰어난; 주목할 만한
Someone or something that is remarkable is unusual or special in a way that makes people notice them and be surprised or impressed.

associate [əsóuʃièit] v. 교제하다, 제휴하다; 연합시키다, 연상하다; n. 동료, 한패
If you associate someone or something with another thing, the two are connected in your mind.

offhand [ɔ́(:)fhǽnd] a. 즉석에서, 준비 없이; 아무렇게나, 무뚝뚝하게
If you say something offhand, you say it without checking the details or facts of it.

predict [pridíkt] v. 예언하다, 예상하다
If you predict an event, you say that it will happen.

14. Dr. Dorian

- **chuckle** [tʃʌ́kl] vi. 낄낄 웃다; n. 낄낄 웃음
  When you chuckle, you laugh quietly.

- **poison** [pɔ́izən] n. 독, 독극물; vt. 독살하다
  Poison is a substance that harms or kills people or animals if they swallow it or absorb it.

- **ivy** [áivi] n. 담쟁이덩굴
  Ivy is an evergreen plant that grows up walls or along the ground.

- **wasp** [wɑsp] n. 장수말벌; 성질 잘 내는 사람
  A wasp is an insect with wings and yellow and black stripes across its body. Wasps have a painful sting like a bee but do not produce honey.

- **relieve** [rilíːv] vt. 안도케 하다, (긴장·걱정 등을) 덜다, 구제하다
  If something relieves an unpleasant feeling or situation, it makes it less unpleasant or causes it to disappear completely.

Let's walk in the Book

1. Why did the crickets sing a song?

  A. They wanted to warn everyone that summer was ending.

  B. They knew that people loved to hear their music.

  C. They liked the weather at the end of the summer and wanted to sing about it.

  D. They wanted to spread the word about happiness and changing of the seasons.

2. Which of the following was NOT true about the end of the summer?

  A. Charlotte knew that she didn't have much time left.

  B. Fern and Avery knew school began soon.

  C. Mrs. Zuckerman was happy that the summer was over.

  D. The young geese knew they wouldn't be little goslings again.

3. Because of the crickets noise _____

  A. more people came to see Wilbur.

  B. Wilbur was fed more often.

  C. the geese dug up potatoes.

  D. the sheep felt uneasy they broke a hole in the fence.

15. The Crickets

4. What did Wilbur do when the crowd became bored watching him?

A. He batted his eyelashes.

B. He did a back flip with a twist.

C. He tilted his head and breathe deeply.

D. He stood on his hind legs and jump up and down.

5. Which of the following was true about Wilbur?

A. Wilbur thought he was better than the other farm animals because he was famous.

B. Wilbur stopped worrying about the future.

C. Wilbur was stuck up and conceited.

D. Wilbur was always modest.

Vocabulary in Charlotte's Web

* **monotonous** [mənátənəs] a. 단조로운, 변화 없는, 지루한
  Something that is monotonous is very boring because it has a regular, repeated pattern which never changes.

* **dusty** [dʌ́sti] a. 먼지투성이의, 먼지 많은
  If places, roads, or other things outside are dusty, they are covered with tiny bits of earth or sand, usually because it has not rained for a long time.

* **frost** [frɔːst] n. 서리; v. 서리로 덮다, 서리가 앉다
  When there is frost or a frost, the temperature outside falls below freezing point and the ground becomes covered in ice crystals.

* **anxiety** [æŋzáiəti] n. 걱정, 근심, 불안
  Anxiety is a feeling of nervousness or worry.

* **admire** [ædmáiər] v. 감탄하다, 탄복하다
  If you admire someone or something, you like and respect them very much.

* **reputation** [rèpjətéiʃən] n. 평판, 명성
  To have a reputation for something means to be known or remembered for it.

* **glow** [glou] v. 빛을 내다; n. 빛, 밝음
  If something glows, it produces a dull, steady light.

* **crowd** [kraud] n. 군중, 인파; v. 군집하다, 붐비다
  A crowd is a large group of people who have gathered together.

  stuck up [stʌkʌp] a. 거드름부리는, 점잔빼는, 거만한
  If you say that someone is stuck up, you mean that are very proud and unfriendly because they think they are very important.

* **modest** [mádist] a. 겸손한, 정숙한; 적당한
  If you say that someone is modest, you approve of them because they do not talk much about their abilities or achievements.

* **fame** [feim] n. 명성, 명예
  If you achieve fame, you become very well-known.

* **spoil** [spɔil] v. 망치다, 못쓰게 만들다
  If you spoil children, you give them everything they want or ask for.

15. The Crickets

mere [miər] a. 단순한, 순전한, 단지 …에 불과한
You use mere to emphasize how unimportant or inadequate something is, in comparison to the general situation you are describing.

confident [kánfidənt] a. 자신만만한; 확신하는
If a person or their manner is confident, they feel sure about their own abilities, qualities, or ideas.

distinguish [distíŋgwiʃ] v. 눈에 띄게 하다; 구별하다, 분별하다
If you distinguish yourself, you do something that makes you famous or important.

inconvenient [ìnkənví:njənt] a. 불편한, 부자유스런; 형편이 마땅치 않은
Something that is inconvenient causes problems or difficulties for someone.

sac [sæk] n. [생물] 주머니, 낭(囊), 액낭(液囊), 기낭(氣囊)
A sac is a small part of an animal's body, shaped like a little bag. It contains air, liquid, or some other substance.

versatile [və́:rsətl] a. 다재다능한, 다방면의, 다용도의
If you say that a person is versatile, you approve of them because they have many different skills.

stunt [stʌnt] n. 묘기, 곡예, 아슬아슬한 재주; v. 묘기를 부리다, 곡예비행을 하다
A stunt is something interesting that is done in order to attract attention and get publicity for the person or company responsible for it.

twitch [twitʃ] n. 홱 잡아당김; vi. 홱 잡아당기다[채다]; (손가락·근육 따위가) 씰룩거리다
A sudden quick movement.

moody [mú:di] a. 침울한, 언짢은; 변덕스러운 (moodily ad. 침울하게)
If you describe something as moody, you mean that it suggests particular emotions, especially sad ones.

forsake [fərséik] vt. 내버리다, 버리고 돌보지 않다
If you forsake someone, you leave them when you should have stayed, or you stop helping them or looking after them.

grasshopper [grǽshàpər] n. 베짱이, 메뚜기
A grasshopper is an insect with long back legs that jumps high into the air and makes a high, vibrating sound.

 **Let's walk in the Book**

1. Match the character with his/her dream:

Avery •   a. Dreamt of getting sick in the swings.

Fern •   b. Dreamt of throwing baseballs at a cloth cat and winning a Navajo blanket.

Lurvy •   c. Dreamt about a deep freeze unit.

Mr. Zuckerman •   d. Dreamt of the Farris wheel stopping and being in the top car.

Mrs. Zuckerman • e. Dreamt about Wilbur winning all of the prizes at the Fair.

2. Why did Fern wear a dress to the Fair?

A. Mrs. Arable made Fern wear a dress.

B. Fern knew that there would be boys at the Fair.

C. Mr. Zuckerman wanted everyone to look their best at the Fair.

D. Fern and Avery would enter a competition and they wanted to look nice.

3. What part of Wilbur's body was dirty?

A. Wilbur's feet were dirty.

B. The backs of Wilbur's legs were dirty.

C. Wilbur's face was dirty.

D. Wilbur was dirty behind his ears.

16. Off to the Fair

4. Why did Templeton decide to go to the Fair?

A. He wanted to find words for Charlotte to write on the web.

B. He wanted to help Wilbur.

C. He wanted to eat the food at the Fair.

D. He wanted to meet other rats at the Fair.

5. Why did Wilbur struggle when Mr. Zuckerman tried to put him in the crate?

A. The old sheep told Wilbur that he would be killed at the Fair.

B. If Wilbur did not struggle, Mr. Zuckerman would think that Wilbur was sick.

C. The animals thought it would be funny to see Mr. Zuckerman struggle with Wilbur.

D. If Wilbur did not struggle, Mr. Zuckerman would think that Wilbur was bewitched.

Vocabulary in Charlotte's Web

Ferris wheel [férishwi:l] n. 대회전식 관람차 (미국의 발명가 이름에서 따옴)
A Ferris wheel is a very large upright wheel with carriages around the edge of it which people can ride in. Ferris wheels are often found at theme parks or funfairs.

swing [swiŋ] n. 그네; 흔들림; v. 흔들다; 매달리다; 빙 돌다
A seat for swinging on, hung from above on ropes or chains.

genuine [dʒénjuin] a. 진짜의, 진품의; 진심의
Genuine is used to describe people and things that are exactly what they appear to be, and are not false or an imitation.

Navajo blanket [nǽvəhòu blǽŋkit] n. 나바호 족이 만든 수공예 담요
Navajo blankets are textiles produced by Navajo people of the Four Corners area of the United States.

deep freeze [di:pfri:z] n. 급속 냉동기 (상표명)
A deep freeze is the same as a freezer.

lug [lʌg] v. 힘껏 끌어당기다; 질질 끌다
If you lug a heavy or awkward object somewhere, you carry it there with difficulty.

scrub [skrʌb] v. 북북 문지르다, 비벼서 씻다; n. 북북 문질러 닦기
If you scrub something, you rub it hard in order to clean it, using a stiff brush and water.

polish [páliʃ] v. 닦다, 윤내다
If you polish something, you rub it with a cloth to make it shine.

straw [strɔ:] n. 짚, 밀짚; 스트로, 빨대
Straw consists of the dried, yellowish stalks from crops such as wheat or barley.

occasion [əkéiʒən] n. 경우, 특별한 일
An occasion is an important event, ceremony, or celebration.

buttermilk [bʌ́tərmìlk] n. 버터마일크 (버터를 빼고 난 우유; 우유를 발효시킨 식품)
Buttermilk is the liquid that remains when fat has been removed from cream when butter is being made.

16. Off to the Fair

* **filthy** [fílθi] a. 불결한, 더러운
  Something that is filthy is very dirty indeed.

* **crust** [krʌst] n. 딱딱한 외피; 빵 껍질
  A crust is a hard layer of something, especially on top of a softer or wetter substance.

smudge [smʌdʒ] n. 더러움, 얼룩; v. 더럽히다; 더러워지다
A smudge is a dirty mark.

* **woodshed** [wúdʃèd] n. 목재 헛간 (wood 나무, 목재 + shed 오두막, 우리)
  A woodshed is a small building which is used for storing wood for a fire.

* **bucket** [bʌ́kit] n. 버킷, 물통; 양동이
  A bucket is a round metal or plastic container with a handle attached to its sides.

* **paddle** [pǽdl] n. 주걱; 노; 탁구 라켓
  A paddle is a short pole with a wide flat part at one end or at both ends.

* **dragline** [drǽglain] n. (기구 등의) 끄는 줄, 유도 로프
  A dragline is a rope used to guide the movement of the load of a crane.

* **trickle** [tríkəl] vi. 똑똑 떨어지다, 졸졸 흐르다; n. 물방울
  When a liquid trickles, or when you trickle it, it flows slowly in very small amounts.

* **shave** [ʃeiv] v. (수염 등을) 깎다, 면도하다; n. 면도 (도구)
  When a man shaves, he removes the hair from his face using a razor or shaver so that his face is smooth.

* **plaid** [plæd] a. 격자무늬의; n. 격자무늬
  Plaid is material with a check design on it.

* **parade** [pəréid] v. 열 지어 행진하다; n. 행렬, 행진
  When people parade somewhere, they walk together in a formal group or a line.

* **tease** [ti:z] v. 놀리다, 희롱하다; n. 끓리기
  To tease someone means to laugh at them or make jokes about them in order to embarrass, annoy, or upset them.

Vocabulary in Charlotte's Web

errand [érənd] n. 심부름, 심부름 가기
An errand is a short trip that you make in order to do a job for someone, for example when you go to a shop to buy something for them.

grumble [grʌ́mbəl] v. 불평하다, 툴툴대다; n. 투덜댐
If someone grumbles, they complain about something in a bad-tempered way.

spill [spil] v. 엎지르다, 흘리다; 누설하다
If a liquid spills or if you spill it, it accidentally flows over the edge of a container.

feast [fi:st] n. 진수성찬; 축제; v. 축연을 베풀다, 진수성찬을 먹다
A feast is a large and special meal.

oat [out] n. 귀리 (오트밀의 원료, 가축의 사료)
The oat is a species of cereal grain grown for its seed.

trot [trɑt] v. 빠른 걸음으로 가다; 총총걸음 치다; n. 빠른 걸음
If you trot somewhere, you move fairly fast at a speed between walking and running, taking small quick step.

pace [peis] v. (규칙적으로) 왔다 갔다 하다; n. 한 발, 걸음; 속도
To walk with regular steps in one direction and then back again.

trample [trǽmpəl] v. 내리밟다, 짓밟다; 무시하다; n. 쿵쿵거리며 걸음, 짓밟음
If someone tramples something or tramples on it, they step heavily and carelessly on it and damage it.

infield [ínfi:ld] n. 농가 주변[부근]의 밭, 경작지; 내야, 내야수
An infield is the area around farm.

foul [faul] a. 더러운, 불결한, 냄새 나는; 비열한, 못된
If you describe something as foul, you mean it is dirty and smells or tastes unpleasant.

hard-boiled [háːrdbɔ́ild] a. 단단하게 삶은; 비정한
A hard-boiled egg has been boiled in its shell until the whole of the inside is solid.

16. Off to the Fair

* **crumb** [krʌm] n. 작은 조각, 빵 부스러기, 빵가루
  Crumbs are tiny pieces that fall from bread, biscuits, or cake when you cut it or eat it.

* **particle** [páːrtikl] n. 극소량, 티끌, 입자
  A particle of something is a very small piece or amount of it.

* **veritable** [vérətəbəl] a. 진실의, 틀림없는, 참된, 진정한
  Used to describe something as another, more exciting, interesting or unusual thing, as a way of emphasizing its character.

* **treasure** [tréʒər] n. 보물, 보배; vt. 소중히 하다; 비축해 두다
  Treasures are valuable objects.

* **fragment** [frǽgmənt] n. 부서진 조각, 파편, 단편
  A fragment of something is a small piece or part of it.

dribble [dríbəl] v. (물방울 따위가) 똑똑 떨어지다; 침을 흘리다; 드리블하다
If a liquid dribbles somewhere, or if you dribble it, it drops down slowly or flows in a thin stream.

candied apple n. 캔디 애플 (막대기에 꽂은 사과에 캐러멜이나 시럽을 입힌 것)
Candied apples are whole apples covered in a hard sugar candy coating.

* **abandon** [əbǽndən] vt. 버리다; 단념하다, 그만두다
  If you abandon a place, thing, or person, you leave the place, thing, or person permanently or for a long time.

fluff [flʌf] n. 보풀, 솜털
Fluff consists of soft threads or fibres in the form of small, light balls or lumps.

popsicle [pápsikəl] n. (가는 막대기에 얼린) 아이스 캔디 (ice lolly의 상표명)
A Popsicle is a piece of flavored ice or ice cream on a stick.

gnaw [nɔː] v. 갉다, 갉아먹다
If people or animals gnaw something or gnaw at it, they bite it repeatedly.

loot [luːt] n. 전리품, 약탈품; 부정이득, 횡령품; v. 약탈하다, 횡령하다
Loot is stolen money or goods.

Vocabulary in Charlotte's Web

* **booth** [buːθ] n. 부스; 노점, 매점
A booth is a small area separated from a larger public area by screens or thin walls.

* **blaze** [bleiz] vi. 타오르다; n. 불꽃, 화염; 섬광
If someone's eyes are blazing with an emotion, or if an emotion is blazing in their eyes, their eyes look very bright because they are feeling that emotion so strongly.

* **appetizing** [ǽpitàiziŋ] a. 식욕을 돋우는, 맛있어 보이는
Appetizing food looks and smells good, so that you want to eat it.

* **yarn** [jɑːrn] n. 모험담, 허풍스런[꾸며낸] 이야기; 직물 짜는 실, 방적사
A yarn is a story that someone tells, often a true story with invented details which make it more interesting.

* **surpass** [sərpǽs] vt. …보다 뛰어나다, 우월하다
If one person or thing surpasses another, the first is better than, or has more of a particular quality than, the second.

* **mash** [mæʃ] n. 짓이긴 것; vt. 짓찧다, 짓이기다
A mash of food is a soft mass of food.

* **scamper** [skǽmpər] vi. 재빨리 달리다, 날쌔게 움직이다; n. 뛰어다님, 질주
When people or small animals scamper somewhere, they move there quickly with small, light steps.

* **crawl** [krɔːl] vi. 기어가다, 느릿느릿 가다; n. 기어감; 서행
When you crawl, you move forward on your hands and knees.

slat [slæt] ① n. 얇은 널빤지, 널조각 ② v. 소리를 내며 부딪치다, 요란스럽게 두드리다; 세차게 던지다
Slats are narrow pieces of wood, metal, or plastic, usually with spaces between them, that are part of things such as Venetian blinds or cupboard doors.

knothole [nάthòul] n. (널판의) 옹이구멍
A knothole is a void left by a knot in the wood.

* **cargo** [kάːrgou] n. (선박이나 비행기의) 화물, 선화, 뱃짐
The goods that are being carried in a ship or plane.

16. Off to the Fair

stowaway [stóuəwèi] n. 밀항자, 무임승차[승선]자
A stowaway is a person who hides in a ship, aeroplane, or other vehicle in order to make a journey secretly or without paying.

alongside [əlɔ́:ŋsàid] ad., prep. …에 옆으로 대고
If one thing is alongside another thing, the first thing is next to the second.

struggle [strʌ́gəl] v. 발버둥치다, 몸부림치다; 분투[고투]하다; n. 발버둥질, 노력
If you struggle when you are being held, you twist, kick, and move violently in order to get free.

tussle [tʌ́səl] n. 격투, 난투; 투쟁, 논쟁; v. 격투하다, 싸우다
If one person tussles with another, or if they tussle, they get hold of each other and struggle or fight.

resist [rizíst] vt. 저항하다, 저지하다
If you resist something such as a change, you refuse to accept it and try to prevent it.

bewitch [biwítʃ] vt. 마법을 걸다, 호리다, 매혹시키다
If someone or something bewitches you, you are so attracted to them that you cannot think about anything else.

pummel [pʌ́məl] vt. (연달아) 주먹으로 치다, 연타하다
If you pummel someone or something, you hit them many times using your fists.

squash [skwɑʃ] ① v. 짓누르다, 으깨다 ② n. 호박
If someone or something is squashed, they are pressed or crushed with such force.

buffet [bʌ́fit] ① v. 치다; 괴롭히다; n. 타격; 시달림, 학대 ② n. 뷔페
If something is buffeted by strong winds or by stormy seas, it is repeatedly struck or blown around by them.

bruise [bru:z] v. 타박상을 주다, 멍들게 하다; n. 타박상, 멍
If you bruise a part of your body, a bruise appears on it, for example because something hits you.

Vocabulary in Charlotte's Web

lacerate [lǽsərèit] vt. 찢다, 찢어내다; 괴롭히다
If something lacerates your skin, it cuts it badly and deeply.

biff [bif] vt. 강타하다; n. 강타
If you biff someone, you hit them with your fist.

* **shove** [ʃʌv] v. 밀치다, 떠밀다, 밀고 나아가다
If you shove someone or something, you push them with a quick, violent movement.

tailgate [téilgèit] n. (트럭·마차·왜건 등의) 뒷문; v. 바싹 따라가다
A tailgate is a door at the back of a truck or car, that is hinged at the bottom so that it opens downwards.

복습 **cheer** [tʃiər] v. 갈채하다, 응원하다; 기운을 북돋우다; n. 환호, 갈채
When people cheer, they shout loudly to show their approval or to encourage someone.

복습 **runt** [rʌnt] n. (한배 새끼 중의) 작은 동물
The runt of a group of animals born to the same mother at the same time is the smallest and weakest of them.

복습 **litter** [lítər] n. (개·돼지 등의) 한배 새끼; 어질러진 물건, 난잡함; vt. 어질러 놓다
A litter is a group of animals born to the same mother at the same time.

복습 **faint** [feint] vi. 기절하다; a. 희미한, 어렴풋한
If you faint, you lose consciousness for a short time.

* **kneel** [ni:l] vi. 무릎 꿇다
When you kneel, you bend your legs so that your knees are touching the ground.

** **rush** [rʌʃ] v. 흐르다; 돌진하다, 서두르다; n. 돌진, 분주한 활동
If air or liquid rushes somewhere, it flows there suddenly and quickly.

this instant idiom 지금 당장에, 그 즉시; 그 자리에서

* **toss** [tɔ:s] v. 던지다; 동요하다, 뒹굴다; n. 던져 올림; 위로 던짐
If you toss something somewhere, you throw it there lightly, often in a rather careless way.

16. Off to the Fair

dash [dæʃ] v. 돌진하다; 내던지다; n. 돌격
If you dash somewhere, you run or go there quickly and suddenly.

emergency [imə́:rdʒənsi] n. 비상사태, 비상시; 위급, 급변
An emergency is an unexpected and difficult or dangerous situation, especially an accident, which happens suddenly and which requires quick action to deal with it.

crouch [krautʃ] v. 몸을 구부리다, 쭈그리다, 웅크리다; n. 웅크림
If you are crouching, your legs are bent under you so that you are close to the ground and leaning forward slightly.

sunstroke [sʌ́nstròuk] n. 일사병, 열사병
Sunstroke is an illness caused by spending too much time in hot sunshine.

brim [brim] v. 넘치다, 넘치려고 하다
If someone or something is brimming with a particular quality, they are full of that quality.

thrash [θræʃ] v. 뒹굴다, 몸부림치다; 마구 때리다
If someone thrashes about, or thrashes their arms or legs about, they move in a wild or violent way.

grunt [grʌnt] vi. (돼지가) 꿀꿀거리다; (사람이) 툴툴거리다; n. 꿀꿀[툴툴]거리는 소리
When an animal grunts, it makes a low rough noise.

heave [hi:v] n. 들어올림; (무거운 것을) 내던짐; v. (들어)올리다; 부풀다
An act of lifting, pulling or throwing.

nail [neil] vt. 못을 박다; n. 손톱, 발톱; 못
If you nail something somewhere, you fix it there using one or more nails.

 **Let's walk in the Book**

1. Which of the following was NOT a rule that Avery and Fern had to follow?
    A. They had to be back at the truck by noon.
    B. They shouldn't eat too much junk food.
    C. They needed to wait for Wilbur to be unloaded before they could go into the Fair.
    D. They should not spend all of their money in the first few minutes.

2. What was a difference between Wilbur's pen at the barn and his pen at the Fair?
    A. Wilbur's pen at the Fair did not have any shade.
    B. Wilbur's pen at the Fair was grassy.
    C. Mr. Zuckerman put clean straw into Wilbur's pen at the Fair.
    D. Wilbur's pen at the Fair did not have a trough.

3. What did Templeton do when they first arrived at the Fair?
    A. Templeton explored the Fairgrounds.
    B. Templeton ate Wilbur's food.
    C. Templeton stayed in the crate.
    D. Templeton went to Uncle's pen.

17. Uncle

4. What did Charlotte say was unattractive about Uncle?

A. Charlotte said that Uncle's size was unattractive.

B. Charlotte said that Uncle's personality was unattractive.

C. Charlotte said that Uncle's weight was unattractive.

D. Charlotte said that Uncle's coat was unattractive.

5. Why did Charlotte think that Uncle was a hard pig to beat?

A. Uncle was not a spring pig and was larger than Wilbur.

B. Uncle had a beautiful and clean coat.

C. Uncle was more pleasant to be around than Wilbur.

D. Uncle was larger and heavier than Wilbur.

Vocabulary in Charlotte's Web

* **sprinkling** [spríŋkliŋ] n. 흩뿌리기, 살포
  A sprinkling of something is a small quantity or amount of it, especially if it is spread over a large area.

* **moisten** [mɔ́isən] v. 축축하게 하다, 축축해지다, 적시다, 젖다
  To moisten something means to make it slightly wet.

  blat [blæt] v. (송아지·양이) 울다; (구어) 떠들썩하게 지껄여대다
  When an animal such as a calf or sheep blats, it cries.

* **enormous** [inɔ́ːrməs] a. 거대한, 막대한
  You can use enormous to emphasize the great degree or extent of something.

* **firework** [fáiərwə̀ːrk] n. 불꽃, 불꽃놀이
  Fireworks are small objects that are lit to entertain people on special occasions.

* **steer** [stiər] v. 조종하다, 키를 잡다
  When you steer a car, boat, or plane, you control it so that it goes in the direction that you want.

* **quarter** [kwɔ́ːrtər] n. 4분의 1달러, 25센트 경화; 4분의 1
  A quarter is an American or Canadian coin that is worth 25 cents.

* **dime** [daim] n. 다임, 10센트 동전 ('잔돈'이라는 뜻이 내포됨)
  A dime is an American or Canadian coin worth ten cents.

* **nickel** [níkəl] n. 5센트짜리 통화; 니켈 (금속 원소 중 하나)
  In the United States and Canada, a nickel is a coin worth five cents.

* **spend** [spend] v. 쓰다, 소비하다
  When you spend money, you pay money for things that you want.

* **pickpocket** [píkpɑ̀kit] n. 소매치기
  A pickpocket is a person who steals things from people's pockets or bags in public places.

* **caution** [kɔ́ːʃən] v. 경고하다, 주의시키다; n. 조심, 신중
  If someone cautions you, they warn you about problems or danger.

17. Uncle

merry-go-round [mérigouràund] n. 회전목마
A merry-go-round is a large circular platform at a fairground on which there are model animals or vehicles for people to sit on or in as it turns round.

excitement [iksáitmənt] n. 흥분 (상태)
You use excitement to refer to the state of being excited, or to something that excites you.

blow [blou] v. (blew-blown) 불다, 바람에 날리다; n. 불기; 강타, 타격
When you blow your nose, you force air out of it through your nostrils in order to clear it.

grassy [grǽsi] a. 풀이 우거진, 풀이 많은; 연초록색의
A grassy area of land is covered in grass.

shed [ʃed] n. 광, (간이) 창고; 오두막
A shed is a small building that is used for storing things such as garden tools.

scramble [skrǽmbəl] v. 기어오르다; 서로 (다투어) 빼앗다; n. 기어오르기
If you scramble over rocks or up a hill, you move quickly over them or up it using your hands to help you.

post [poust] ① n. 기둥, 말뚝 ② n. 우편; 우체국; vt. 우송하다 ③ n. 지위, 직
A post is a strong upright pole made of wood or metal that is fixed into the ground.

roof [ru:f] n. 지붕; 최고부, 꼭대기
The roof of a building is the covering on top of it that protects the people and things inside from the weather.

skim milk [skimmilk] n. 탈지 우유 (지방 함량을 0.1% 이내로 줄인 우유)
Skim milk is milk that contains less fat than normal because the cream has been removed from it.

purebred [pjúərbréd] a. 순혈종의
A purebred animal is one whose parents and ancestors all belong to the same breed.

Vocabulary in Charlotte's Web

beam [bi:m] n. 들보, 도리; 광선 v. 빛을 발하다; 밝게 미소 짓다
A beam is a long thick bar of wood, metal, or concrete, especially one used to support the roof of a building.

hearty [há:rti] a. 마음에서 우러난, 원기 왕성한; 풍부한; 건강한
Hearty people or actions are loud, cheerful, and energetic.

ascend [əsénd] v. 올라가다, 오르다
If something ascends, it moves up.

claim [kleim] vt. 주장하다; 요구하다, 청구하다; n. 요구, 청구
If you say that someone claims that something is true, you mean they say that it is true.

unattractive [ʌ̀nətrǽktiv] a. 애교 없는; 눈을 끌지 않는, 흥미 없는
If you describe something as unattractive, you mean that people do not like it and do not want to be involved with it.

personality [pə̀:rsənǽləti] n. 개성, 성격
Your personality is your whole character and nature.

crack [kræk] v. (농담 등을) 하다, 날카로운 소리가 나게 하다; 금이 가다; n. 갈라진 금; 갑작스런 날카로운 소리
If you crack a joke, you tell it.

on account of idiom …의 이유로, …때문에
On account of something means because of something.

swollen [swóulən] a. 부어오른, 부푼; 과장한, 과대한
If a part of your body is swollen, it is larger and rounder than normal, usually as a result of injury or illness.

listless [lístlis] a. …할 마음이 없는, 열의 없는; 무관심한, 냉담한
Someone who is listless has no energy or enthusiasm.

weary [wíəri] a. 피로한, 지친 (wearily ad. 지쳐서, 지친 상태로)
If you are weary, you are very tired.

nap [næp] n. 낮잠, 선잠; v. 잠깐 졸다, 선잠 자다
If you have a nap, you have a short sleep, usually during the day.

17. Uncle

silky [sílki] a. 비단 같은, 보드라운, 매끄러운, 광택 있는
If something has a silky texture, it is smooth, soft, and shiny, like silk.

fierce [fiərs] a. 맹렬한; 흉포한, 사나운 (fiercely ad. 사납게, 맹렬하게)
Fierce conditions are very intense, great, or strong.

Cracker jack [krǽkərdʒæ̀k] n. 당밀로 뭉쳐 놓은 팝콘
Cracker Jack is a snack consisting of caramel-coated popcorn and peanuts.

fan [fæn] vt. 부채질하다; 부채꼴로 펴다; n. 부채, 선풍기
If you fan yourself or your face when you are hot, you wave a fan or other flat object in order to make yourself feel cooler.

lunch box [lʌ́ntʃbɑks] n. 도시락
A lunch box is a small container with a lid, which you put food such as sandwiches in it to eat for lunch at work or at school.

sideboard [sáidbɔ̀:rd] n. 측면부; (식당의 벽 쪽에 비치된) 찬장, 식기대
A sideboard of something is a part forming a side of it.

stretch out phrasal v. 팔다리를 뻗다; (…을 잡으려고) 손을 뻗다
If you stretch out or stretch yourself out, you lie with your legs and body in a straight line.

Let's walk in the Book

1. What did Fern do with Henry Fussy at the Fair?

A. She rode the swings with him.

B. She rode the Farris wheel with him.

C. She introduced Henry to Wilbur.

D. She rode on the merry-go-round with him.

2. How did Templeton find the new word for the web?

A. He tore the word from a deep freezer advertisement.

B. He tore the word from a hot dog package.

C. He tore the word from a folded newspaper.

D. He tore the word from a magazine article.

3. Why was humble a good word for the web?

A. Wilbur was a proud pig.

B. Wilbur enjoyed getting attention from the people at the Fair.

C. Wilbur was not proud and he was near the ground.

D. Wilbur was satisfied with the Fair.

4. Which of the following did NOT happen at night?

A. There were fireworks at the Fair.

B. The Arables and the Zuckermans went home.

C. Templeton went exploring.

D. The people at the Fair saw Charlotte's web.

18. The Cool of the Evening

5. Why didn't Wilbur feel homesick at night?

A. The people from the Fair were around his pen.

B. Charlotte was with him.

C. Templeton was eating food near him.

D. He was too excited for the next day to be homesick.

Vocabulary in Charlotte's Web

creep [kri:p] vi. (crept-crept) 기다, 살금살금 걷다; n. 포복
When people or animals creep somewhere, they move quietly and slowly.

crate [kreit] n. 나무 상자
A crate is a large box used for transporting or storing things.

keen [ki:n] a. 열심인, 열중하는, 열망하는
You use keen to indicate that someone has a lot of enthusiasm for a particular activity and spends a lot of time doing it.

detect [ditékt] vt. 발견하다, 간파하다
If you detect something, you notice it or sense it.

explore [iksplɔ́:r] v. 탐험하다, 탐사하다, 조사하다
If you explore a place, you travel around it to find out what it is like.

mumble [mʌ́mbəl] v. 중얼[웅얼]거리다; 우물우물 씹다; n. 중얼거림
If you mumble, you speak very quietly and not at all clearly with the result that the words are difficult to understand.

messenger boy [mésəndʒərbɔi] n. 사환, 심부름꾼
A messenger boy is a boy who is employed to take messages to people.

crackle [krǽkəl] n., v. 우지직우지직[딱딱] 소리 (내다)
A series of short sharp sounds.

beano [bi:nou] (= beanfeast) n. (영) (1년에 한 번) 즐거운 잔치; 고용인에게 베푸는 잔치
A party or celebration.

refresh [rifréʃ] vt. 원기를 회복하다; 상쾌하게 하다
If something refreshes you when you have become hot, tired, or thirsty, it makes you feel cooler or more energetic.

starry [stá:ri] a. 별이 많은[반짝이는], 반짝반짝 빛나는
A starry night or sky is one in which a lot of stars are visible.

leftover [léftòuvər] n. 나머지, 찌꺼기; a. 나머지의, 남은
You can refer to food that has not been eaten after a meal as leftovers.

18. The Cool of the Evening

deviled [dévəld] a. 맵게 양념한
Deviled food is highly spiced food.

★ **core** [kɔːr] n. (배·사과 등의) 응어리, 과심(果心); (사물의) 핵심; a. 핵심의
The core of a fruit is the central part of it.

wormy [wə́ːrmi] a. 벌레 먹은; 벌레 붙은, 벌레가 많은
If something is wormy, it contains many worms, or infected or damaged by worms.

복습 **clipping** [klípiŋ] n. (신문·잡지의) 오려낸 기사; 가위질, 깎기
A clipping is an article, picture, or advertisement that has been cut from a newspaper or magazine.

‡ **humble** [hʌ́mbəl] a. 겸손한, 겸허한; 천한, 비천한
A humble person is not proud and does not believe that they are better than other people.

★ **sneer** [sniər] v. 비웃다, 냉소하다; n. 비웃음, 냉소
If you sneer at someone or something, you express your contempt for them by the expression on your face or by what you say.

복습 **fetch** [fetʃ] vt. 가져오다, 데려오다, 불러오다
If you fetch something or someone, you go and get them from the place where they are.

‡ **deliver** [dilívər] v. 배달하다, 넘겨주다; (연설·설교를) 하다; 분만[해산]하다
If you deliver something somewhere, you take it there.

복습 **grin** [grin] v. 이를 드러내고 싱긋 웃다; n. 싱긋 웃음
When you grin, you smile broadly.

thee [ðiː] (고·시어) (thou의 목적격) 너를[에게]
A word meaning 'you', used when talking to only one person who is the object of the verb.

복습 **scheme** [skiːm] n. 계획; 음모; v. 계획을 세우다; 음모를 꾸미다 (schemer n. 음모가)
A scheme is someone's plan for achieving something.

Vocabulary in Charlotte's Web

* **vanish** [vǽniʃ] v. 사라지다, 자취를 감추다
If someone or something vanishes, they disappear suddenly.

** **scatter** [skǽtə:r] v. 흩뿌리다, 뿌리다; 폭발하다; n. 흩뜨림, 흩뜨려진 것
To throw or drop things in different directions so that they cover an area of ground.

grandstand [grǽndstænd] n. (경마장·경기장 등의) 특별 관람석
A grandstand is a covered stand with rows of seats for people to sit on at sporting events.

forkful [fɔ́:rkfùl] n. 한 포크 분
You can refer to an amount of food on a fork as a forkful of food.

* **pat** [pæt] v. 가볍게 두드리다, 토닥거리다
If you pat something or someone, you tap them lightly, usually with your hand held flat.

* **homesick** [hóumsìk] a. 향수병의, 고향을 그리워하는
If you are homesick, you feel unhappy because you are away from home and are missing your family, friends, and home very much.

** **own** [oun] vt. 소유하다; 지배하다; a. 자신의, 고유한
If you own something, it is your property.

복습 **sparrow** [spǽrou] n. 참새
A sparrow is a small brown bird which is common in towns and cities.

복습 **stir** [stə:r] v. 움직이다; 휘젓다; n. 휘젓기, 뒤섞음
If you stir, you move slightly, for example because you are uncomfortable or beginning to wake up.

복습 **rattle** [rǽtl] v. 덜거덕거리며 움직이다; n. 덜거덕거리는 소리
When something rattles or when you rattle it, it makes short sharp knocking sounds because it is being shaken or it keeps hitting against something hard.

복습 **rooster** [rú:stər] n. 수탉
A rooster is an adult male chicken.

18. The Cool of the Evening

* **crow** [krou] ① vi. (수탉이) 울다; n. 수탉의 울음소리 ② n. 까마귀
When a cock (= an adult male chicken) crows, it makes a very long and loud sharp cry.

* **fade** [feid] vi. 희미해지다, 바래다, 시들다
When a colored object fades or when the light fades it, it gradually becomes paler.

* **whisper** [hwíspər] v. 속삭이다, 작은 목소리로 말하다; n. 속삭임
When you whisper, you say something very quietly, using your breath rather than your throat.

* **masterpiece** [mǽstərpìːs] n. 걸작, 명작
A masterpiece is an extremely clever or skilful example of something.

* **canned** [kænd] a. 통조림 처리한
When food or drink is canned, it is put into a metal container and sealed so that it will remain fresh.

* **tuck** [tʌk] v. 밀어 넣다, 쑤셔 넣다; n. 접어 넣은 단
If you tuck something somewhere, you put it there so that it is safe, comfortable, or neat.

Let's walk in the Book

1. **Which of the following was NOT true about Charlotte's egg sac?**

   A. It was be waterproof.

   B. It was made of a tough material.

   C. It couldn't hold many eggs.

   D. It kept the eggs warm and dry.

2. **Why was Charlotte sad when talking about her egg sac?**

   A. She didn't want to have many children.

   B. She knew that she wouldn't meet her children.

   C. She didn't think that her egg sac was made well enough to last until spring.

   D. She was exhausted from making her egg sac.

3. **How did Charlotte feel after making her egg sac?**

   A. She felt weak.

   B. She felt excited about her egg sac.

   C. She felt peaceful.

   D. She felt scared.

19. The Egg Sac

4. Why was Charlotte disgusted with Templeton?
   A. Templeton was being rude to Charlotte.
   B. Templeton didn't care about Charlotte's egg sac.
   C. Templeton ate too much food at the Fair.
   D. Templeton lied about Uncle winning first prize.

5. Who still had high spirits after seeing the first prize ribbon on Uncle's pen?
   A. Mrs. Zuckerman   B. Mrs. Arable
   C. Lurvy   D. Mr. Zuckerman

Vocabulary in Charlotte's Web

‡ automobile [ɔ́:təməbì:l] n. 자동차
An automobile is a car.

cocoon [kəkú:n] n. (누에) 고치; 안식처
A cocoon is a covering of silky threads that the larvae of moths and other insects make for themselves before they grow into adults.

cotton candy [kɑ́tnkæ̀ndi] n. 솜사탕
Cotton candy is a large pink or white mass of sugar threads that is eaten from a stick.

nifty [nífti] a. 멋진, 재치 있는
If you describe something as nifty, you think it is neat and pleasing or cleverly done.

magnum opus [mǽgnəmóupəs] n. 대작, 대표작, 최고 걸작
A magnum opus is the greatest or most important work produced by a writer, artist, musician, or academic.

‡ construct [kənstrʌ́kt] vt. 건설하다, 조립하다; n. 구조물
If you construct something such as a building, road, or machine, you build it or make it.

‡ guarantee [gæ̀rəntí:] vt. 보증하다, 확실히 하다; n. 보증, 담보물
If one thing guarantees another, the first is certain to cause the second thing to happen.

‡ tough [tʌf] a. 강인한, 질긴; 거친; 고단한, 고된
A tough substance is strong, and difficult to break, cut, or tear.

★ waterproof [wɔ́tərprù:f] a. 방수의, 물이 새어 들지 않는; n. 방수복; 방수재료
Something which is waterproof does not let water pass through it.

★ down-hearted [daun-hɑ́:rtid] a. 낙담한
If you are down-hearted, you are feeling sad and discouraged.

pep [pep] n. 원기, 기력; vt. 원기를 북돋우다, 격려하다
Pep is liveliness and energy.

19. The Egg Sac

* **languish** [læŋgwiʃ] vi. 기운이 없어지다, 시들다; 동경하다, 그리워하다
  If something languishes, it is not successful, often because of a lack of effort or because of a lot of difficulties.

** **bother** [báðər] v. 괴롭히다, 귀찮게 하다, 폐 끼치다
  If something bothers you, or if you bother about it, it worries, annoys, or upsets you.

복습 **dew** [dju:] n. 이슬; 신선함, 상쾌함; v. 이슬로 적시다; 축이다, 눅눅하게 하다
  Dew is small drops of water that form on the ground and other surfaces outdoors during the night.

복습 **strand** [strænd] ① n. 가닥, 외가닥으로 꼰 끈 ② v. 좌초시키다; 오도 가도 못하다
  A strand of something such as hair, wire, or thread is a single thin piece of it.

** **marvel** [má:rvəl] v. 놀라다, 경탄하다; n. 놀라운 일, 경이
  If you marvel at something, you express your great surprise, wonder, or admiration.

복습 **whisker** [hwískər] n. 수염, 구레나룻
  The whiskers of an animal such as a cat or a mouse are the long stiff hairs that grow near its mouth.

* **husky** [háski] ① a. 쉰 목소리의; 껍질의 ② n. 에스키모 개
  If someone's voice is husky, it is low and rather rough, often in an attractive way.

** **jar** [dʒɑ:r] n. 항아리, 단지, 병
  A jar is a glass container with a lid that is used for storing food.

* **hoarse** [hɔ:rs] a. 목쉰, 쉰 목소리의 (hoarsely ad. 쉰 목소리로)
  If your voice is hoarse, your voice sounds rough and unclear.

  carouse [kəráuz] v. 마시고 떠들다, 대음하다; n. 주연, 술잔치, 흥청거림
  If you say that people are carousing, you mean that they are behaving very noisily and drinking a lot of alcohol as they enjoy themselves.

* **gorge** [gɔ:rdʒ] n. 포식, 대식; 골짜기; v. 배불리 먹다, 포식하다
  To eat lots of something in a very greedy way.

Vocabulary in Charlotte's Web

ripen [ráipən] vi. (과일 등이) 익다; 익히다, 원숙하게 하다
When crops ripen or when the sun ripens them, they become ripe.

seasoned [síːzənd] a. 양념한
If food is seasoned, it cooked with salt, pepper, or spices.

passage [pǽsidʒ] n. 경과, 추이; 통행, 통로; 여행
The passage of a period of time is its passing.

ashamed [əʃéimd] a. 부끄러워, 수치스러워
If someone is ashamed, they feel embarrassed or guilty because of something they do or they have done.

acute [əkjúːt] a. 급성의; 격렬한; 예리한
An acute illness is one that becomes severe very quickly but does not last very long.

indigestion [ìndidʒéstʃən] n. 소화 불량, 소화가 안 됨
If you have indigestion, you have pains in your stomach and chest that are caused by difficulties in digesting food.

snarl [snɑːrl] v. 으르렁거리다; 고함[호통]치다; n. 으르렁거림
When an animal snarls, it makes a deep rough sound in its throat while showing its teeth.

lick [lik] v. 이기다; 핥다; 스치다; n. 핥기
If you lick someone or something, you easily defeat them in a fight or competition.

hanker [hǽŋkər] vi. 갈망[열망]하다, 동경하다
If you hanker after something, you want it very much.

pork [pɔːrk] n. 돼지고기
Pork is meat from a pig, usually fresh and not smoked or salted.

smoked [smoukt] a. 훈제한, 그을린
If fish or meat is smoked, it is hung over burning wood so that the smoke preserves it and gives it a special flavor.

19. The Egg Sac

stuff [stʌf] vt. 채우다, 채워 넣다; n. 물질, 성분, 재료, 본질
If you stuff yourself, you eat a lot of food.

bloat [blout] vt. 부풀게 하다, 팽창시키다; 자부하다, 우쭐하게 하다
If something bloats, it swells or makes something swell, especially in an unpleasant way.

dopey [dóupi] a. 마취된 것 같은, 멍한; 멍청한, 지루한
Someone who is dopey is sleepy, as though they have been drugged.

suspicious [səspíʃəs] a. (…을) 의심하는, 의심스러운
(suspiciously ad. 의심스러운 눈초리로)
If you are suspicious of someone or something, you do not trust them, and are careful when dealing with them.

congratulation [kəngrætʃəléiʃən] n. 축하, 경하
You say 'Congratulations' to someone in order to congratulate them on something nice that has happened to them or something good that they have done.

rejoice [ridʒɔ́is] v. 기뻐하다, 즐겁게 하다
If you rejoice, you are very pleased about something and you show it in your behavior.

gaze [geiz] vi. 뚫어지게 보다, 응시하다; n. 응시, 주시
If you gaze at someone or something, you look steadily at them for a long time.

grateful [gréitfəl] a. 감사하는, 고마운; 기분 좋은; 반가운
If you are grateful for something that someone has given you or done for you, you have warm, friendly feelings towards them and wish to thank them.

handkerchief [hǽŋkərtʃif] n. 손수건
A handkerchief is a small square piece of fabric which you use for blowing your nose.

stableboy [stéiblbɔ̀i] n. 마부 (특히 소년)
A stableboy is a young man who works in a stable looking after the horses.

Vocabulary in Charlotte's Web

trickle [tríkəl] vi. 똑똑 떨어지다, 졸졸 흐르다; n. 물방울
When a liquid trickles, or when you trickle it, it flows slowly in very small amounts.

passer-by [pǽsərbái] n. (pl. passers-by) 통행인, 지나가는 사람
A passer-by is a person who is walking past someone or something.

bystander [báistændər] n. 구경꾼, 방관자; 관계없는 사람
A bystander is a nonparticipant spectator.

prompt [prɑmpt] a. 신속한, 재빠른; 즉석의; vt. 자극하다 (promptly ad. 신속히, 즉시)
A prompt action is done without any delay.

unable [ʌnéibəl] a. …할 수 없는; 무력한, 무능한, 자격[권한]이 없는
If you are unable to do something, it is impossible for you to do it.

yell [jel] v. 소리치다; n. 고함, 부르짖음
If you yell, you shout loudly, because you are excited, angry, or in pain.

flutter [flʌ́tər] vi. 퍼덕거리다, 날개 치며 날다
If something thin or light flutters, or if you flutter it, it moves up and down or from side to side with a lot of quick, light movements.

confetti [kənféti(ː)] n. 색종이 조각 (축제일 등에 뿌리는)
Confetti is small pieces of colored paper that people throw over the bride and bridegroom at a wedding.

crouch [krautʃ] v. 몸을 구부리다, 쭈그리다, 웅크리다; n. 웅크림
If you are crouching, your legs are bent under you so that you are close to the ground and leaning forward slightly.

encircle [ensə́ːrkl] vt. 에워[둘러]싸다; n. 에워쌈, 포위
To encircle something or someone means to surround or enclose them, or to go round them.

weary [wíəri] a. 피로한, 지친
If you are weary, you are very tired.

19. The Egg Sac

content [kəntént] vt. 만족을 주다, 만족시키다; a. 만족하여; n. 내용물, 내용; 만족 (contented a. 만족한)
Pleased with your situation and not needing or desiring it to be better.

snap [snæp] v. 날카롭게[느닷없이] 말하다; 홱 잡다, 짤깍 소리 내다; n. 툭 소리 냄
If someone snaps at you, they speak to you in a sharp, unfriendly way.

commotion [kəmóuʃən] n. 동요; 소동, 소요
A commotion is a lot of noise, confusion, and excitement.

bury [béri] vt. 묻다, 파묻다, 매장하다
To bury something means to put it into a hole in the ground and cover it up with earth.

boost [buːst] vt. 밀어올리다; 후원하다, 부양하다; 밀어올림
If one thing boosts another, it causes it to increase, improve, or be more successful.

aboard [əbɔ́ːrd] ad. 타고, 승선하여
If you are aboard a ship or plane, you are on it or in it.

topmost [tápmòust] a. 최고의, 최상(급)의
The topmost thing in a number of things is the one that is highest or nearest the top.

 **Let's walk in the Book**

1. How did Templeton feel about Wilbur getting an award?

A. Templeton thought that Wilbur receiving an award was nonsense.

B. Templeton was excited for Wilbur.

C. Templeton didn't care about Wilbur getting an award and didn't watch the event.

D. Templeton agreed that Wilbur was a special pig.

2. What did Fern do before Wilbur received the award?

A. She cleaned behind Wilbur's ears and gave him a buttermilk bath.

B. She stood next to Wilbur excited about the special award.

C. She went looking for Henry so they could ride the Ferris wheel.

D. She cleaned up her clothes and brushed her hair so she would look nice for the award ceremony.

3. Which of the following was NOT said by the loudspeaker during the award ceremony?

A. Wilbur attracted many tourists to the state.

B. Charlotte was a clever spider and she was complimented for her writing in the web.

C. The people should feel proud and grateful for experiencing Wilbur and the web.

D. Wilbur was a good looking pig.

20. The Hour of Triumph

4. What did Mr. Zuckerman win?

   A. He won a special silver medal and $20.
   B. He won a special plaque engraved by the governors of the Fair.
   C. He won a special bronze medal and $25.
   D. He won a gold medal and a blue ribbon.

5. Why did Wilbur win a medal at the County Fair?

   A. Wilbur attracted many visitors to the County Fair.
   B. Wilbur was the heaviest and most radiant pig at the Fair.
   C. Wilbur was voted the best spring pig at the County Fair.
   D. Wilbur attracted supernatural forces to the County Fair.

Vocabulary in Charlotte's Web

* **pompous** [pámpəs] a. 점잔 빼는, 거드름 피우는
  If you describe someone as pompous, you mean that they behave or speak in a very serious way because they think they are more important than they really are.

* **bear** [bɛər] ① vt. 나르다; 지탱하다; 낳다 ② n. 곰
  If you bear something somewhere, you carry it there or take it there.

* **extraordinary** [ikstrɔ́:rdənèri] a. 비상한, 비범한, 예사롭지 않은
  If you describe something as extraordinary, you mean that it is very unusual or surprising.

* **approach** [əpróutʃ] v. …에 다가가다, 가까이 가다; 다가오다; n. 접근
  When you approach something, you get closer to it.

* **proceed** [prousí:d] vi. 속행하다, 계속하다; 나아가다, 가다
  If an activity, process, or event proceeds, it goes on and does not stop.

* **dizzy** [dízi] a. 현기증 나는, 어지러운; 아찔한
  If you feel dizzy, you feel as if everything is spinning round and being unable to balance.

* **run over** phrasal v. (차가) …을 치다, (사람이) 차로 …을 치다
  If a vehicle or its driver runs a person or animal over, it knocks them down or drives over them.

* **tailgate** [téilgèit] n. (트럭·마차·왜건 등의) 뒷문; v. 바싹 따라가다
  A tailgate is a door at the back of a truck or car, that is hinged at the bottom so that it opens downwards.

* **disgust** [disgʌ́st] n. 싫음, 혐오감; vt. 역겹게 하다, 넌더리나게 하다
  (in disgust idiom 싫증나서, 넌더리나서)
  Disgust is a feeling of very strong dislike or disapproval.

* **duck** [dʌk] ① v. 머리를 홱 숙이다; 물속으로 들어가다 ② n. 오리
  If you duck, you move your head or the top half of your body quickly downwards to avoid something that might hit you, or to avoid being seen.

20. The Hour of Triumph

boom [bu:m] vi. (소리가) 쿵 하고 울리다; 활기를 띠우다, 붐이 일다
When something such as someone's voice, a cannon, or a big drum booms, it makes a loud, deep sound that lasts for several seconds.

fuss [fʌs] n. 야단법석, 호들갑; 몸달아 설침, 흥분
Fuss is anxious or excited behavior which serves no useful purpose.

embrace [embréis] vt. 껴안다, 포옹하다
If you embrace someone, you put your arms around them and hold them tightly, usually in order to show your love or affection for them.

courage [kə́:ridʒ] n. 용기, 담력
Courage is the quality shown by someone who decides to do something difficult or dangerous, even though they may be afraid.

triumph [tráiəmf] n. 승리, 대성공; vi. 성공하다, 이기다
A triumph is a great success or achievement, often one that has been gained with a lot of skill or effort.

clap [klæp] v. (손뼉을) 치다, 가볍게 두드리다
When you clap, you hit your hands together to show appreciation or attract attention.

dirt [də:rt] n. 진흙; 쓰레기; 흙
If there is dirt on something, there is dust, mud, or a stain on it.

stroke [strouk] ① vt. 쓰다듬다, 어루만지다; n. 쓰다듬기, 달램 ② n. 타격, 일격; 발작
If you stroke someone or something, you move your hand slowly and gently over them.

unique [ju:ní:k] a. 유일한, 독특한
Something that is unique is the only one of its kind.

recall [rikɔ́:l] vt. 상기하다, 생각나게 하다; n. 회상
When you recall something, you remember it and tell others about it.

ordinary [ɔ́:rdənèri] a. 보통의, 평범한
Something that is out of the ordinary is unusual or different.

Vocabulary in Charlotte's Web

all and sundry idiom 누구 할 것 없이, (각자) 모두, 저마다
All and sundry means everyone.

phenomenon [finámənàn] n. 현상
A phenomenon is something that is observed to happen or exist.

supernatural [sù:pərnǽtʃərəl] a. 초자연의, 불가사의한
Supernatural creatures, forces, and events are believed by some people to exist or happen, although they are impossible according to scientific laws.

blush [blʌʃ] v. 얼굴을 붉히다, (얼굴이) 빨개지다; n. 얼굴을 붉힘, 홍조
When you blush, your face becomes redder than usual because you are ashamed or embarrassed.

magnificent [mægnífəsənt] a. 웅장한, 장엄한, 훌륭한
If you say that something or someone is magnificent, you mean that you think they are extremely good, beautiful, or impressive.

terrific [tərífik] a. 굉장한, 빼어난; 무서운
If you describe something or someone as terrific, you are very pleased with them or very impressed by them.

spotless [spátlis] a. 흠 없는, 오점이 없는
spot (n. 얼룩, 반점) + less (suf. 없는)

snout [snaut] n. (돼지 등의) 코, 주둥이
The snout of an animal such as a pig is its long nose.

whence [hwens] ad. 어떻게, 왜, 어찌하여; 어디로부터
Whence means from what place, source, or cause.

on behalf of idiom …을 대신하여, 대표하여; …을 위하여
If you do something on someone's behalf, you do it for that person as their representative.

suitable [sú:təbəl] a. (…에) 적당한, 어울리는, 알맞은 (suitably ad. 적당히, 상당히)
Someone or something that is suitable for a particular purpose or occasion is right or acceptable for it.

20. The Hour of Triumph

* **engrave** [engréiv] vt. 조각하다, 새기다; 명심하다, 새겨두다
  If you engrave something with a design or words, or if you engrave a design or words on it, you cut the design or words into its surface.

* **token** [tóukən] n. 표시; 징후, 증거; 토큰
  If you give something to a person or do something for them as a token of your feelings, you give it or do it as a way of expressing those feelings.

* **appreciation** [əprì:ʃiéiʃən] n. 감사; 감상, 음미
  Appreciation of something is the recognition and enjoyment of its good qualities.

* **compliment** [kámpləmənt] n. 찬사, 칭찬의 말; v. 경의를 표하다, 칭찬하다
  (complimentary a. 칭찬하는)
  A compliment is a polite remark that you say to someone to show that you like their appearance, appreciate their qualities, or approve of what they have done.

* **collapse** [kəlǽps] v. 쓰러지다, 맥없이 주저앉다; 무너지다; n. 무너짐, 붕괴
  If you collapse, you suddenly faint or fall down because you are very ill or weak.

* **blank** [blæŋk] a. 멍한, 얼빠진, 공허한; 공백의; n. 공백
  If you look blank, your face shows no feeling, understanding, or interest.

* **unconscious** [ʌnkánʃəs] a. 의식[정신]을 잃은; 모르는, 알아채지 못하는
  Someone who is unconscious is in a state similar to sleep, usually as the result of a serious injury or a lack of oxygen.

* **holler** [hálər] v. 고함지르다, 외치다; n. 외침, 고함
  If you holler, you shout loudly.

* **bite** [bait] v. 물다, 물어뜯다; 깨물다; n. 묾, 물기
  To use your teeth to cut into something or someone.

* **revive** [riváiv] v. 되살리다, 소생하게 하다
  If you manage to revive someone who has fainted or if they revive, they become conscious again.

Vocabulary in Charlotte's Web

flash [flæʃ] n. 순간; 번쩍임, 번쩍하는 빛; v. 번쩍 비추다; 휙 지나가다
You talk about a flash of something when you are saying that it happens very suddenly and unexpectedly.

hesitate [hézətèit] v. 주저하다, 머뭇거리다, 망설이다
If you hesitate, you do not speak or act for a short time, usually because you are uncertain, embarrassed, or worried about what you are going to say or do.

dash [dæʃ] v. 돌진하다; 내던지다; n. 돌격
If you dash somewhere, you run or go there quickly and suddenly.

splash [splæʃ] v. (물·흙탕물 등을) 튀기다; n. 물 튀기기, 첨벙 (물 튀기는 소리)
If you splash water, you hit or disturb the water in a noisy way, causing some of it to fly up into the air.

soak [souk] v. 적시다, 빨아들이다; 젖다, 스며들다; n. 적심 (soaking a. 흠뻑 젖는)
If a liquid soaks something or if you soak something with a liquid, the liquid makes the thing very wet.

for goodness' sake idiom 제발, 아무쪼록, 부디
For goodness' sake is an exclamation showing surprise, impatience, or some other emotion.

bellow [bélou] vi. 큰 소리로 울다; 고함지르다
If someone bellows, they shout angrily in a loud, deep voice.

drench [drentʃ] vt. 흠뻑 젖게 하다
To drench something or someone means to make them completely wet.

ail [eil] vt. 괴롭히다, 고통을 주다
If something ails someone, they are ill.

meek [mi:k] a. 순한, 유순한, 온순한 (meekly ad. 온순하게)
If you describe a person as meek, you think that they are gentle and quiet, and likely to do what other people say.

roar [rɔ:r] vi. 고함치다, 외치다, 으르렁거리다
If someone roars, they shout something in a very loud voice.

20. The Hour of Triumph

* **tickle** [tíkəl] vt. 재미나게 하다; 간질이다; n. 간지럼
  If something tickles you, it amuses or pleases you.

※ **immediate** [imí:diət] a. 즉각적인, 직접적인 (immediately ad. 곧, 즉각)
  An immediate result, action, or reaction happens or is done without any delay.

* **clown** [klaun] n. 어릿광대; 익살꾼; vi. 익살부리다, 어릿광대짓 하다
  A clown is a performer in a circus who wears funny clothes and bright make-up, and does silly things in order to make people laugh.

※ **imaginary** [imǽdʒənèri] a. 상상의, 가공의
  An imaginary person, place, or thing exists only in your mind or in a story, and not in real life.

armpit [á:rmpìt] n. 겨드랑이
  Your armpits are the areas of your body under your arms where your arms join your shoulders.

※ **applause** [əplɔ́:z] n. 박수갈채, 칭찬
  Applause is the noise made by a group of people clapping their hands to show approval.

calm down phrasal v. 가라앉다; 가라앉히다
  If things calm down, or someone or something calms things down, the amount of activity, trouble, or panic is reduced.

※ **trousers** [tráuzərz] n. (남자용) 바지
  Trousers are a piece of clothing that you wear over your body from the waist downwards, and that cover each leg separately.

 Let's walk in the Book

1. **Which of the following was NOT true after Wilbur received the award?**
   A. Charlotte felt peaceful.
   B. Charlotte felt confident that Wilbur would be safe in the future.
   C. Charlotte felt successful.
   D. Charlotte felt anxious.

2. **Why did Charlotte do so much for Wilbur?**
   A. Wilbur was a friend to her.
   B. She wanted Wilbur to become famous.
   C. She felt like a mother to Wilbur.
   D. She wanted people to know that spiders were smarter than they thought.

21. Last Day

3. What would Wilbur do for Charlotte?

   A. He would give her the award that he won.

   B. He would give his life for her.

   C. He would carry her back to the barn.

   D. He would give her any food she wanted from his trough.

4. Why did Templeton refuse to help Wilbur at first?

   A. He ate too much and his stomach was too full to move.

   B. He thought that saving Charlotte's egg sac was a silly idea.

   C. He was annoyed that nobody showed him appreciation for his work.

   D. He didn't think he could help Wilbur before the people showed up.

5. How did Wilbur convince Templeton to help him?

   A. Wilbur promised Templeton that he would give Templeton first choice in food from the trough everyday.

   B. Wilbur promised Templeton that he would show him more appreciation for his work.

   C. Wilbur told Templeton that he would not be allowed into the crate without helping him.

   D. Wilbur promised Templeton that all of the barn animals would respect him and give him their food if he helped.

Vocabulary in Charlotte's Web

* **strain** [strein] n. 긴장, 피로; 팽팽함; v. 분투하다; 잡아당기다, 긴장시키다
Strain is a state of worry and tension caused by a difficult situation.

* **assure** [əʃúər] vt. 보증하다, 안심시키다
If you assure someone that something is true or will happen, you tell them that it is definitely true or will definitely happen, often in order to make them less worried.

* **secure** [sikjúər] a. 안전한, 위협이 없는; v. 안전하게 하다, 확보하다
If you are secure, you are safe from harm or attack.

* **harm** [hɑːrm] vt. 해치다, 손상을 입히다; n. 해, 손해
To harm a person or animal means to cause them physical injury, usually on purpose.

* **pasture** [pǽstʃər] n. 목장, 목초지
Pasture is land with grass growing on it for farm animals to eat.

* **pond** [pɑnd] n. 못; 늪; 샘물
A pond is a small area of water that is smaller than a lake.

* **precious** [préʃəs] a. 귀중한, 가치가 있는, 비싼
If something is precious to you, you regard it as important and do not want to lose it.

* **deserve** [dizə́ːrv] vt. …을 할[받을] 만하다, …할 가치가 있다
If you say that a person or thing deserves something, you mean that they should have it or receive it because of their actions or qualities.

* **tremendous** [tribméndəs] a. 거대한, 대단한; 엄청난, 무서운
You use tremendous to emphasize how strong a feeling or quality is, or how large an amount is.

* **mess** [mes] n. 엉망진창, 난잡함; v. 어질러놓다; 망쳐놓다
If you say that something is a mess or in a mess, you think that it is in an untidy state.

* **trifle** [tráifəl] n. 하찮은 것, 사소한 일; 조금, 약간
A trifle is something that is considered to have little importance, value, or significance.

21. Last Day

generous [dʒénərəs] a. 관대한, 아끼지 않는, 후한
A generous person is friendly, helpful, and willing to see the good qualities in someone or something.

sentiment [séntəmənt] n. 감정, 정서; 감정적인 생각
A sentiment that people have is an attitude which is based on their thoughts and feelings.

spinneret [spínərèt] n. (거미·누에 등의) 방적 돌기 (실이 나오는 구멍)
A spinneret is a spider's silk-spinning organ.

agony [ǽgəni] n. 고민, 고뇌, 고통
Agony is great physical or mental pain.

sorrow [sárou] n. 슬픔, 비애
Sorrow is a feeling of deep sadness or regret.

sob [sɑb] n. 흐느낌, 오열; v. 흐느껴 울다
A sob is one of the noises that you make when you are crying.

rack [ræk] vt. 괴롭히다, 고통을 주다; n. 선반, (모자·옷 등의) 걸이
If someone is racked by something such as illness or anxiety, it causes them great suffering or pain.

heave [hiːv] v. 올라가다, 높아지다; (무거운 것을) 들어 올리다
If something heaves, it moves up and down with large regular movements.

desolation [dèsəléiʃən] n. 쓸쓸함, 외로움; 황량
Desolation is a feeling of great unhappiness and hopelessness.

moan [moun] v. 신음하다, 끙끙대다; n. 신음
If you moan, you make a low sound, usually because you are unhappy or in pain.

make a scene idiom 소란을 피우다, 야단법석을 떨다
Make a scene means complaining noisily or behaving badly.

thrash [θræʃ] v. 뒹굴다, 몸부림치다; 마구 때리다
If someone thrashes about, or thrashes their arms or legs about, they move in a wild or violent way.

Vocabulary in Charlotte's Web

ridiculous [ridíkjələs] a. 터무니없는; 웃기는, 우스꽝스러운
If you say that something or someone is ridiculous, you mean that they are very foolish.

make sense idiom 도리에 맞다; 뜻이 통하다
If something makes sense, it is a sensible thing to do.

deserted [dizə́:rtid] a. 인적이 끊긴; 사람이 살지 않는
A deserted place is a place with no people in it.

panic [pǽnik] n. 공황, 패닉; v. 당황하다, 허둥대다
Panic is a very strong feeling of anxiety or fear, which makes you act without thinking carefully.

toss [tɔ:s] v. 던지다; 동요하다, 뒹굴다; n. 던져 올림; 위로 던짐
If you toss something somewhere, you throw it there lightly, often in a rather careless way.

monkeyshine [mʌ́ŋkiʃàin] n. 짓궂은 장난, 놀림
A monkeyshine is a trick or prank.

growl [graul] v. 으르렁거리다, 고함치다; n. 으르렁거리는 소리
When a dog or other animal growls, it makes a low noise in its throat, usually because it is angry.

yawn [jɔ:n] vi. 하품하다; n. 하품, 입을 크게 벌림
If you yawn, you open your mouth very wide and breathe in more air than usual, often when you are tired or when you are not interested in something.

rescue [réskju:] n. 구출, 구원; vt. 구조하다, 구출하다
Rescue is help which gets someone out of a dangerous or unpleasant situation.

imitate [ímitèit] vt. 모방하다, 흉내 내다; 따르다, 본받다
If you imitate someone, you copy what they do or produce.

abuse [əbjú:z] n. 욕설, 독설; 남용, 오용; 학대; vt. 남용하다, 학대하다
Abuse is extremely rude and insulting things that people say when they are angry.

21. Last Day

wisecrack [wáizkræ̀k] n. 재치 있는[비꼬는] 말
A wisecrack is a clever remark that is intended to be amusing, but is often rather unkind.

desperation [dèspəréiʃən] n. 필사적임; 절망, 자포자기
Desperation is the feeling that you have when you are in such a bad situation that you will try anything to change it.

attitude [ǽtitjùːd] n. 태도, 몸가짐
Your attitude to something is the way that you think and feel about it, especially when this shows in the way you behave.

relaxation [rìːlækséiʃən] n. 휴양, 편히 쉼; 이완
Relaxation is a way of spending time in which you rest and feel comfortable.

mimic [mímik] vt. 흉내 내다, 흉내 내어 조롱하다
If you mimic the actions or voice of a person or animal, you imitate them, usually in a way that is meant to be amusing or entertaining.

touching [tʌ́tʃiŋ] a. 감동시키는, 감동적인
If something is touching, it causes feelings of sadness or sympathy.

fond [fɑnd] a. 좋아하는, 정다운 (fondness n. 애호)
If you are fond of something, you like it or you like doing it very much.

solemn [sɑ́ləm] a. 엄숙한, 근엄한
Someone or something that is solemn is very serious rather than cheerful or humorous.

cross one's heart idiom (가슴에 십자를 긋고) 맹세하다
If you say 'cross my heart', you emphasize that you are telling the truth or will do what you promise.

bare [bɛər] v. (이빨 등을) 드러내다, 노출시키다; a. 발가벗은, 있는 그대로의
If you bare something, you uncover it and show it.

snip [snip] v. 싹둑 베다, (가위로) 자르다; n. 싹둑 자름, 가위질
If you snip something, or if you snip at or through something, you cut it quickly.

Vocabulary in Charlotte's Web

thread [θred] n. 실, 바느질 실; vt. 실을 꿰다
Thread or a thread is a long very thin piece of a material such as cotton, nylon, or silk.

extreme [ikstríːm] a. 극단의, 극도의; n. 극단, 극단적인 것
Extreme means very great in degree or intensity.

adrift [ədríft] ad., a. (사물이) 풀리어, 표류하여, 떠돌고; (정처 없이) 헤매어, 방황하여
If something comes adrift, it is no longer attached to an object that it should be part of.

spool [spuːl] n. 실감개, 실패; v. 실패에 감다
A spool is a round object onto which thread, tape, or film can be wound, especially before it is put into a machine.

bundle [bʌ́ndl] n. 묶음, 다발, 꾸러미; vt. 다발[꾸러미]로 하다, 묶다, 싸다
A bundle of things is a number of them that are tied together or wrapped in a cloth or bag so that they can be carried or stored.

waterproof [wɔ́ːtərprùːf] a. 방수의 n. 방수복, 레인코트
That does not let water through or that cannot be damaged by water.

drool [druːl] vi. 침을 흘리다; n. 허튼 소리, 두서없는 말
If a person or animal drools, saliva drops slowly from their mouth.

summon [sʌ́mən] vt. 내다, 불러일으키다; 소환하다, 호출하다
If you summon a quality, you make a great effort to have it.

van [væn] n. 소형 운반차[트럭]
A van is a small or medium-sized road vehicle with one row of seats at the front and a space for carrying goods behind.

belonging [bilɔ́(ː)ŋiŋ] n. 소유물, 소지품
Your belongings are the things that you own, especially things that are small enough to be carried.

trailer [tréilər] n. (자동차 등의) 트레일러; 끄는 사람; 예고편
A trailer is the long rear section of a lorry or truck, in which the goods are carried.

21. Last Day

* **forlorn** [fərlɔ́:rn] a. 버려진, 버림받은; 고독한, 쓸쓸한
  If a place is forlorn, it is deserted and not cared for, or has little in it.

* **litter** [lítər] vt. 어질러 놓다; n. (개·돼지 등의) 한배 새끼; 어질러진 물건, 난잡함
  If a number of things litter a place, they are scattered untidily around it or over it.

 **Let's walk in the Book**

1. After the Fair, what did Fern think about all the time?

A. She thought about Wilbur winning the special award at the Fair.

B. She thought about the time she had on the Ferris wheel with William Fussy.

C. She thought about the next county Fair.

D. She thought about spending time in the barn with Wilbur.

2. Why did Templeton get so fat?

A. He didn't exercise and spent all of his time inside the barn.

B. He ate too much food from Wilbur's trough.

C. He stole a lot of food from inside the house.

D. Lurvy fed Templeton three meals a day.

3. What did Wilbur do to the egg sac?

A. He tried to keep it warm with his breath at night.

B. He placed it where Charlotte's web used to be.

C. He warmed the egg sac with his nose during the daytime.

D. He regularly pressed on the egg sac to try and make the eggs hatch faster.

22. A Warm Wind

4. Which of the following did NOT happen when spring came?

A. The animals heard baby frogs in the evening.

B. There were new baby animals on the farm.

C. The animals felt the warm wind blow.

D. Lurvy took down Charlotte's old web.

5. What happened when Wilbur said hello to the newly hatched spiders?

A. The little spiders ignored Wilbur.

B. They nodded their heads at Wilbur.

C. They said hello but Wilbur couldn't hear them.

D. They each made a balloon and sailed away.

Vocabulary in Charlotte's Web

- **nail** [neil] n. 못; 손톱, 발톱; vt. 못을 박다
  A nail is a thin piece of metal with one pointed end and one flat end.

- **strand** [strænd] ① n. 가닥, 외가닥으로 꼰 끈 ② v. 좌초시키다; 오도 가도 못하다
  A strand of something such as hair, wire, or thread is a single thin piece of it.

- **lump** [lʌmp] n. 덩어리, 덩이; 다량, 듬뿍
  A lump of something is a solid piece of it.

- **squash** [skwɑʃ] ① n. 호박 ② v. 짓누르다, 으깨다
  A type of vegetable that grows on the ground.

- **nip** [nip] vt. 시들게 하다, 얼게[상하게] 하다; 물다, 집다, 꼬집다
  To harm or damage something.

- **frosty** [frɔ́:sti] a. 서리가 내리는, 혹한의; 냉담한, 쌀쌀한
  If the weather is frosty, the temperature is below freezing.

- **maple** [méipəl] n. 단풍나무
  A maple or a maple tree is a tree with five-pointed leaves which turn bright red or gold in autumn.

- **birch** [bə:rtʃ] n. 박달나무, 자작나무
  A birch or a birch tree is a type of tall tree with thin branches.

- **gnaw** [nɔ:] v. 갉다, 갉아먹다
  If people or animals gnaw something or gnaw at it, they bite it repeatedly.

- **sniff** [snif] v. 코를 킁킁거리다, 냄새를 맡다
  When you sniff, you breathe in air through your nose hard enough to make a sound.

- **plow** [plau] v. (밭을) 갈다, 경작하다; n. 쟁기
  When someone plows an area of land, they turn over the soil.

- **drift** [drift] n. (눈·비·토사 등의) 바람에 날려 쌓인 것; 표류, 흐름; v. 표류하다, 떠돌다
  A large pile of something, especially snow, made by the wind.

- **sled** [sled] n. 썰매
  A sled is a vehicle which can slide over snow.

22. A Warm Wind

coast [koust] v. 썰매로 미끄러져 내려가다, 관성으로 달리다; n. 연안, 해안
If a vehicle coasts somewhere, it continues to move there with the motor switched off, or without being pushed or pedalled.

retort [ritɔ́:rt] v. 반박하다, 말대꾸하다; n. 말대꾸, 반박
To retort means to reply angrily to someone.

thermometer [θərmámitər] n. 온도계
A thermometer is an instrument for measuring temperature.

bleak [bli:k] a. 황폐한, 쓸쓸한; 냉혹한
If you describe a place as bleak, you mean that it looks cold, empty.

lee [li:] n. 바람이 닿지 않는[없는] 곳, 가려진 곳, 그늘; 바람이 불어가는 쪽
The lee of a place is the shelter that it gives from the wind or bad weather.

turnip [tə́:rnip] n. 순무(의 뿌리)
A turnip is a round vegetable with a greenish-white skin that is the root of a crop.

chilly [tʃíli] a. 차가운, 쌀쌀한; 냉담한
Something that is chilly is unpleasantly cold.

cozy [kóuzi] a. 기분 좋은, 포근한; 화기애애한
A house or room that is cozy is comfortable and warm.

grain [grein] n. 곡물, 낟알; 미량
Grain is a cereal crop, especially wheat or corn, that has been harvested and is used for food or in trade.

rag [ræg] n. 넝마, 걸레
A rag is a piece of old cloth which you can use to clean or wipe things.

trinket [tríŋkit] n. 자질구레한 장신구; 시시한 것
A trinket is a pretty piece of jewellery or small ornament that is inexpensive.

keepsake [kí:psèik] n. 기념품, 유품
A keepsake is a small present that someone gives you so that you will not forget them.

Vocabulary in Charlotte's Web

gigantic [dʒaigǽntik] a. 거대한, 막대한
If you describe something as gigantic, you are emphasizing that it is extremely large in size, amount, or degree.

woodchuck [wúdtʃʌ̀k] n. (북미산의) 마멋 (다람쥣과 마멋속의 포유동물을 통틀어 이르는 말)
A woodchuck is a small animal with short legs and rough, reddish brown fur, which lives in North America.

sneer [sniər] v. 비웃다, 냉소하다; n. 비웃음, 냉소
If you sneer at someone or something, you express your contempt for them by the expression on your face or by what you say.

satisfaction [sæ̀tisfǽkʃən] n. 만족, 만족을 주는 것
Satisfaction is the pleasure that you feel when you do something or get something that you wanted or needed to do or get.

scoop [sku:p] vt. 퍼 올리다, 푸다, 뜨다; n. 국자, 주걱
If you scoop a person or thing somewhere, you put your hands or arms under or round them and quickly move them there.

cock [kɑk] v. 위로 치올리다, (귀·꽁지를) 쫑긋 세우다; n. 수탉; 마개, 꼭지
If you cock a part of your body in a particular direction, you lift it or point it in that direction.

shrill [ʃril] a. (소리가) 날카로운, 새된, 높은
A shrill sound is high-pitched and unpleasant.

ditch [ditʃ] n. 수로, 도랑; v. 도랑을 파다, 해자로 두르다
A ditch is a long narrow channel cut into the ground at the side of a road or field.

chatter [tʃǽtər] vi. (시냇물이) 졸졸 흐르다; 재잘거리다; 달각달각 소리 내다; n. 수다
If objects chatter, they make short repeated sounds.

streaky [strí:ki] a. 줄 있는, 줄무늬진; 신경질적인
Something that is streaky is marked with long stripes that are a different color to the rest of it.

22. A Warm Wind

breast [brest] n. 가슴, 가슴 부분
A person's breast is the upper part of his or her chest.

float [flout] v. 뜨다; 띄우다
If something or someone is floating in a liquid, they are in the liquid, on or just below the surface, and are being supported by it.

tan [tæn] a. 황갈색의; vt. (피부를) 햇볕에 태우다; n. 햇볕에 그을음
Something that is tan is a light brown color.

tremble [trémbəl] v. 떨다, 떨리다
If you tremble, you shake slightly because you are frightened or cold.

pound [paund] v. 마구 치대[두드리다], 연타[난타]하다; 맹포격하다; n. 타격, 연타
If you pound something or pound on it, you hit it with great force, usually loudly and repeatedly.

squeal [skwi:l] v. 깩깩거리다, 비명을 지르다; n. 꽥꽥거리는 소리
If someone or something squeals, they make a long, high-pitched sound.

manure [mənjúər] n. 비료, 거름, 퇴비; vt. (땅에) 비료를[거름을] 주다
Manure is animal faeces, sometimes mixed with chemicals, that is spread on the ground in order to make plants grow healthy and strong.

flip [flip] n. 공중제비; 가볍게 침; v. (손가락으로) 튀기다, 확 뒤집다
A movement in which the body turns over in the air.

plant [plænt] vt. 찌르다; 심다; 놓다, 앉히다; n. 식물; 공장
If you plant something somewhere, you put it there firmly.

trail [treil] v. 끌다, 추적하다; n. 끌고 간 자국, 흔적
If you trail something or it trails, it hangs down loosely behind you as you move along.

draft [dræft] n. 틈새 바람, 외풍; 도안, 설계도; vt. 밑그림을 그리다, 설계하다
A draft is a current of air that comes into a place in an undesirable way.

damp [dæmp] a. 축축한, 습기 찬; n. 습기
Something that is damp is slightly wet.

Vocabulary in Charlotte's Web

* **spruce** [spru:s] n. [식물] 가문비나무, 전나무
A spruce is a kind of evergreen tree.

updraft [ʌ́pdræft] n. 기류의 상승 (운동)
An updraft is a strong upward air current.

* **frantic** [fræntik] a. 광란의, 미친 듯 날뛰는
If you are frantic, you are behaving in a wild and uncontrolled way because you are frightened or worried.

복습 **aeronaut** [ɛ́ərənɔ̀:t] n. 기구[비행선] 조종사
An aeronaut is the pilot of a lighter-than-air aircraft, especially a balloon.

복습 **balloonist** [bəlú:nist] n. (스포츠·취미로) 기구 타는 사람
A balloonist is a person who flies a hot-air balloon.

‡ **mist** [mist] n. 안개; v. 안개가 끼다, 눈이 흐려지다
Mist consists of a large number of tiny drops of water in the air, which make it difficult to see very far.

복습 **dreary** [dríəri] a. 적적한, 쓸쓸한, 음울한 (drearily ad. 쓸쓸하게)
If you describe something as dreary, you mean that it is dull and depressing.

복습 **salutation** [sæ̀ljətéiʃən] n. 인사; (가벼운) 절, 경례
Salutation or a salutation is a greeting to someone.

* **definite** [défənit] a. 확정된, 일정한; 명확한 (definitely ad. 확실히, 명확히)
If something such as a decision or an arrangement is definite, it is firm and clear, and unlikely to be changed.

‡ **initial** [iníʃəl] n. 머리글자; a. 처음의, 최초의
Initials are the capital letters which begin each word of a name.

복습 **fancy** [fænsi] ① a. 장식적인, 화려한 ② n. 공상, 홀연히 내킨 생각; v. 공상하다
If you describe something as fancy, you mean that it is special, unusual, or elaborate.

‡ **dumb** [dʌm] a. 우둔한, 어리석은; 말 못하는, 말을 하지 않는
If you say that something is dumb, you think that it is silly and annoying.

22. A Warm Wind

- **dainty** [déinti] a. 섬세한, 가냘픈; 까다로운; 맛이 좋은; n. 맛있는 것, 진미
  (daintily ad. 우아하게; 섬세하게)
  If you describe a movement, person, or object as dainty, you mean that they are small, delicate, and pretty.

- **orb** [ɔːrb] n. 구, 원; vt. 공 모양으로 만들다, 둥글게 하다
  An orb is something that is shaped like a ball, for example the sun or moon.

- **brim** [brim] v. 넘치다, 넘치려고 하다
  If someone or something is brimming with a particular quality, they are full of that quality.

- **hallowed** [hǽloud] a. 신성한, 존경받는
  Hallowed is used to describe something that is respected and admired, usually because it is old, important, or has a good reputation.

- **devote** [divóut] vt. 바치다, 전적으로 쏟다
  If you devote yourself, your time, or your energy to something, you spend all or most of your time or energy on it.

- **owe** [ou] vt. 빚지고 있다, …의 은혜를 입고 있다
  If you owe money to someone, they have lent it to you and you have not yet paid it back.

- **brilliant** [bríljənt] a. 훌륭한, 멋진; 빛나는
  A brilliant person, idea, or performance is extremely clever or skilful.

- **treasure** [tréʒər] vt. 소중히 하다; 비축해 두다; n. 보물, 보배
  If you treasure something that you have, you keep it or care for it carefully because it gives you great pleasure and you think it is very special.

- **pledge** [pledʒ] vt. 맹세하다, 서약하다; n. 맹세, 서약; 저당, 담보; 보증
  When someone pledges to do something, they promise in a serious way to do it.

- **gnat** [næt] n. [곤충] 각다귀 (피를 빨아 먹는 작은 곤충)
  A gnat is a very small flying insect that bites people and usually lives near water.

Vocabulary in Charlotte's Web

* **tranquil** [trǽŋkwil] a. 조용한, 평온한, 평화로운
Something that is tranquil is calm and peaceful.

avoid [əvɔ́id] vt. 피하다, 회피하다
If you avoid something unpleasant that might happen, you take action in order to prevent it from happening.

hatch [hætʃ] v. (알이) 깨다, 부화하다; (음모·계획을) 꾸미다
When an egg hatches or when a bird, insect, or other animal hatches an egg, the egg breaks open and a baby comes out.

dull [dʌl] a. 단조롭고 지루한, 활기 없는; 무딘, 둔한
If you describe someone or something as dull, you mean they are not interesting or exciting.

garrulous [gǽrjələs] a. 수다스러운, 말 많은; (시내 따위) 소리 내며 흐르는
If you describe someone as garrulous, you mean that they talk a great deal, especially about unimportant things.

passage [pǽsidʒ] n. 통행, 통로; 여행; 경과, 추이
A passage through a crowd of people or things is an empty space that allows you to move through them.

glory [glɔ́:ri] n. 영광; vi. 기뻐하다, 자랑으로 여기다
Glory is the fame and admiration that you gain by doing something impressive.

in a class by itself[oneself] idiom 비길 데 없는, 뛰어난
To be something of such a high quality that nothing can be compared to it.

Comprehension Quiz Answers

1. Before Breakfast
1. B
2. D
3. A
4. A
5. C

2. Wilber
1. C
2. C
3. A
4. A
5. C

3. Escape
1. B
2. D
3. A
4. A
5. B

4. Loneliness
1. A
2. D
3. C
4. B
5. B

5. Charlotte
1. C
2. A
3. C
4. B
5. B-A-D-C

6. Summer Days
1. D
2. A
3. A
4. C
5. B

7. Bad News
1. A
2. C
3. A
4. C
5. D

8. A Talk at Home
1. A
2. D
3. D
4. C
5. C

9. Wilbur's Boast
1. D
2. A
3. B
4. B
5. B

10. An Explosion
1. C
2. B
3. C
4. C
5. A

11. The Miracle
1. D
2. B
3. A
4. C
5. C

12. A Meeting
1. B
2. C
3. D
4. D
5. A

13. Good Progress
1. C
2. D
3. A
4. B
5. C

14. Dr. Dorian
1. C
2. D
3. C
4. B
5. C

15. The Crickets
1. A
2. C
3. D
4. D
5. D

16. Off to the Fair

1. Avery - d
   Fern - a
   Lurvy - b
   Mr. Zuckerman - e
   Mrs. Zuckerman - c
2. B
3. D
4. C
5. D

17. Uncle

1. C
2. B
3. C
4. B
5. D

18. The Cool of the Evening

1. B
2. C
3. C
4. D
5. B

19. The Egg Sac

1. C
2. B
3. A
4. C
5. D

20. The Hour of Triumph

1. A
2. C
3. B
4. C
5. A

21. Last Day

1. D
2. A
3. B
4. C
5. A

22. A Warm Wind

1. B
2. B
3. A
4. D
5. C

Index

A

abandon 137
aboard 49, 161
abuse 174
acrobat 109
acute 158
address 56
adjourn 110
admire 74, 130
adore 26, 78
adrift 176
adventure 96
advertisement 109
advice 125
advise 85, 120, 184
affectionate 92
agony 173
ail 168
alder 116
all and sundry 166
all in all 105
allow 34
aloft 124
alongside 27, 139
amount 18
amuse 28
anaesthetic 74
ancient 71
announcement 69
anxiety 130
anxious 69
appall 70
appeal 40, 109
appetite 22, 126
appetizing 138
applause 169
appreciation 167
approach 20, 164
appropriate 56
armpit 169
arrange 29
ascend 114, 146
ashamed 158
asparagus 37, 102
assemble 110
associate 126
assure 172
astonish 116
astride 98
attitude 175
attraction 105
automobile 156
average 111
avoid 49, 186
awful 38
ax 18
axle 32

B

back and forth 86
bake 47
balloonist 120, 184
bare 175
barely 40
barn 29, 54
barrel 41
bathing suit 28
be along 21
bead 70, 102
beam 93, 146
beano 150
bear 164
beard 125
beechnut 86
beetle 60
beg 57, 88
bellow 168
belonging 176
beloved 96
below 115
beneath 114
bestir 99
bewilder 103
bewitch 139
bib 26
biff 140
bill 70
birch 180
bite 167
bitter 48
blank 167
blanket 27
blat 144
blaze 138
bleak 181
blissful 22
bloat 159
bloodthirsty 61
blossom 26
blow 145
blunder 59, 104
blush 23, 56, 166

board 35
boast 82
bold 62
boom 165
boost 161
booth 138
bore 110
bother 157
bottom 93
bough 67
bowl 124
breast 183
breeze 32
brief 67
brilliant 185
brim 141, 185
brisk 75
brook 28, 66
bruise 139
brutal 62
buckboard 105
bucket 34, 135
budge 47, 120
buffet 139
buggy 105
bump 84
bundle 87, 176
burst 75
bury 45, 97, 161
butcher 75
buttermilk 134
by oneself 48
bystander 160

C

call the roll 108
calm down 169
campaign 74
candied apple 137
canned 153
capital 22
captivity 40
capture 95
cargo 138
carouse 157
carriage 27
carton 19
catch on 22
caution 144
cautious 50
ceiling 56, 118
cellar 29, 78, 108
centipede 60
charge 22
chase 37
chatter 182
cheat 55
cheek 19
cheer 39, 140
chest 115
chief 110
chilly 181
chirp 120
chronicle 115
chubby 83
chuckle 35, 54, 83, 127
civil 126
claim 146

clap 165
clasher 54
clever 61
cling 117
clipping 110, 151
clover 62
clown 169
coach 83
coast 181
cock 182
cocker spaniel 37
cockroach 60
cocoon 156
collapse 167
come in handy 96
comfort 40
commotion 37, 161
complaint 96
compliment 167
compunction 70
concern 111
confetti 160
confident 131
congratulation 159
conscience 70
conspiracy 75
construct 156
content 161
core 151
cotton candy 156
courage 165
cousin 119
coxa 82
cozy 181

crack 146
Cracker jack 147
crackle 150
crafty 49
cramped 69
crank 117
crash 94
crate 115, 150
crawl 27, 59, 138
creep 49, 84, 109, 150
cricket 60, 120
crisis 93
crisp 117
crochet 125
crook 44
cross one's heart 175
crouch 84, 141, 160
crow 153
crowd 130
cruel 61
crumb 137
crunchy 117
crust 45, 135
cud 50
cunning 49
curiosity 88, 124
curl 84
custard 45

D

daddy longlegs 60
dagger 20
dainty 185
daisy 92
damp 19, 183
dandelion 68
dare 108
dash 141, 168
dawn 55
daylight 21
daze 39
decency 70
decent 54
deep freeze 134
definite 184
dejected 50
delay 89
delectable 86
delicate 82, 102
deliver 151
deny 58
descend 99, 114
deserted 174
deserve 172
desolation 173
desperation 175
destiny 110
destroy 54
detect 150
determine 56
detest 59
deviled 151
devote 185
dew 115, 157
dig 27
dime 144
dirt 46, 165
discard 34, 116

discourage 95
discover 62
disgust 56, 164
dishmop 116
dishpan 93
distinct 103
distinguish 131
distribute 21
disturb 57
ditch 182
dive 59
dizzy 94, 164
do away with 18
dodge 38, 120
doily 125
doorway 26
dopey 159
doubt 62, 126
down-hearted 156
downhill 39
downspout 44
doze 55
dozen 54, 102
draft 183
dragline 83, 135
drainboard 92
dreadful 59
dreamy 22
dreary 50, 184
drench 168
dribble 137
drift 180
drip 44, 102
drool 97, 176

drowse 99
duck 164
dud 69
dull 95, 186
dumb 184
dump 47
dung 121
dust 125
dusty 130

E
eaves 44
edge 28
effort 69
8-penny nail 41
embarrassment 86
embrace 165
emergency 141
enchant 27, 125
encircle 160
engrave 167
enormous 144
errand 55, 136
excitement 62, 145
exertion 103
explore 150
explosion 95
exterior 62
extra 104
extraordinary 164
extreme 176

F
fade 153
faint 55, 78, 140
fame 130
fan 147
fancy 58, 184
fascinate 124
fasten 85
fatten 74
fear 94
feast 136
feather 61
feed 26
fellow 109
femur 82
fence 35
Ferris wheel 134
fetch 41, 118, 151
fib 124
fidget 126
fierce 62, 147
filthy 135
fin 120
firework 144
firm 29
flake 118
flash 168
flashy 58
flibbertigibbet 48
flip 119, 183
float 183
fluff 137
flutter 160
foggy 102
fold 45
fond 84, 175

for goodness' sake 168
forkful 152
forlorn 177
forsake 131
foul 136
foundation 114
fragment 137
frantic 184
freezer 117
Frigidaire 68
frolic 48
frost 130
frosty 180
furious 59
furthermore 115
fuss 40, 165

G
gabble 96
gain 74
gallop 118
gamble 62
gander 39, 58
garrulous 186
gasp 59
gaze 26, 92, 159
generous 173
genuine 134
get in touch with (sb/sth) 56
gigantic 182
giggle 23
gingersnap 98
glance 83

glare 108
gleam 55
glisten 102
gloomy 61
glory 186
glow 130
glutton 49
gnat 60, 185
gnaw 49, 137, 180
goose 34
gorge 157
gosling 48
grab 22, 39
grain 32, 181
grandstand 152
grass 18
grasshopper 60, 131
grassy 145
grateful 159
gratify 69
gravy 46
graze 44
grease 32
greeting 58
grin 79, 151
groan 47, 93
growl 174
gruff 110
grumble 118, 136
grunt 27, 84, 97, 141
guarantee 156
gullible 92
gulp 97
gumdrop 58

gush 44
gyromatic transmission 104

H
hallowed 185
handkerchief 159
hang 86
hanker 158
hard-boiled 136
harm 172
harness 32
hasty 83
hatch 48, 186
haul 66
hay 32
hayloft 94
hearty 98, 146
heave 141, 173
heel 28
henhouse 93
hesitate 83, 168
hind 39
hinge 116
hire 37
hitch 66
hoarse 157
hoe 105
hoghouse 18
hoist 67
holler 29, 167
homesick 152
hominy 46
honest 47
honk 22, 39

hullabaloo 40
humble 151
hurl 83
hurray 108
husky 157
hysteric 75

I
idiosyncrasy 108
imaginary 169
imagination 79
imitate 174
immediate 37, 169
impress 109
in a class by itself[oneself] 186
incessant 126
inconvenient 131
indigestion 158
infant 21
infield 136
inheritance 60
initial 184
injustice 19
innocent 41
instinct 109
instruction 125
intend 61
interlude 68
interrupt 87
invent 124
itch 35, 94
ivy 127

J

jar 157
jello 98
jelly roll 98
journey 27, 115
jubilee 67
junky 71

K

keen 150
keepsake 181
kneel 140
knot 93
knothole 138

L

label 118
lacerate 140
lack 85
ladder 33
lair 71
lamb 38
lane 44
languish 157
lash 28, 120
lawn 33
leaky 117
leap 119
leave enough 88
ledge 56
lee 181
leftover 45, 98, 150
lick 57, 158
lid 20
lift 20
lilac 66
listless 146
litter 19, 140, 177
loathe 74
loft 32, 67
loot 137
loyal 63
lug 134
lullaby 120
lump 180
lunch box 147
lung 115
lure 40

M

magnificent 166
magnum opus 156
make a scene 173
make sense 174
manure 29, 57, 83, 183
maple 45, 180
marmalade 47
marvel 157
mash 88, 138
masterpiece 153
meadow 45
meek 57, 168
mend 37
mention 47
merciless 120
mercy 92
mere 62, 131
merry 48
merry-go-round 145
mess 172
messenger boy 150
metatarsus 82
middling 40, 97
midge 60
midnight 54
milk of (human) kindness 70
mimic 175
minister 104
miraculous 105
miserable 20, 60, 96
mist 184
moan 75, 173
modest 130
moist 28
moisten 144
molasses 50
monkey wrench 33
monkeyshine 174
monotonous 130
moody 98, 131
moral 70
morsel 46
moth 60
motionless 92
mow 66
mower 33
multiply 61
mumble 126, 150
murmur 103
mutter 71, 103
mysterious 56

N

nail 14, 180
nap 146
narrow 95
Navajo blanket 134
near-sighted 58
neat 102
nectar 68
neglect 85
nerve 88
nest 34
nickel 144
niece 104
nifty 156
nip 180
nipple 21
noble 117
nod 78
nonsense 57
notice 22
notion 104
nudge 71
numerous 61
nursing bottle 21

O

oat 36, 136
objectionable 57
oblige 84
occasion 50, 134
occur 103
offhand 126
on account of 146
on behalf of 166
ooze 29
orb 114, 185
orchard 36, 116
ordinary 103, 165
overall 116
overhead 51
overlook 35
owe 185
own 152

P

pace 96, 136
paddle 135
pail 33, 110
panic 174
parade 135
pardon 57
paring 46
particle 137
passage 158, 186
passer-by 160
pasture 94, 172
pat 152
patch 37, 102
patella 82
patience 69
patient 32, 92
pause 36, 89
peer 27
pen 38
pep 156
personality 146
perspire 32
pester 74
phenomenon 166
phoebe 67
pickpocket 144
pigpen 33
pigweed 44
pile 29
piper 88
pitch 32, 66
pitch fork 33, 115
pitcher 18
plaid 135
plant 183
plaster 19
playmate 124
pledge 185
plenty 109
plot 61
plow 37, 180
pluck 75
plunge 59
poison 127
poke 27, 50, 68, 124
polish 134
pompous 164
pond 172
pop 21
popover 40
popsicle 137
pork 158
possession 97
post 145
pound 70, 183
pour 50, 97
praise 41, 108

prance 36
precious 172
predict 126
prepare 105
preshrunk 118
pretend 78
prick up 38
principal 105
private 49
proceed 108, 164
produce 114
prompt 21, 160
property 54
prove 63, 105
provender 46
prune 46
pry 97
pummel 139
punish 105
pupil 22
purebred 145

Q

quarter 144
Queensborough Bridge 86
queer 19, 36, 78, 104
quit 55, 85
quiver 110

R

race 75
rack 173
racket 37, 54
radial 114
radiant 118
radish 36
rag 116, 181
raisin 45
rake 66
ramble on 78
raspberry 94
rattle 51, 104, 152
rear 59, 84
recall 165
reconsider 41
recover 84
refresh 150
regard 125
rejoice 159
relaxation 175
relieve 127
remark 108
remarkable 126
reputation 130
rescue 174
resist 96, 139
retort 181
revive 167
rid 21
ridiculous 174
rifle 20
rigid 74
rind 98
rip 114
ripe 105
ripen 158
risk 35

roar 168
rodent 70
romp 119
roof 44, 145
rooster 39, 152
root 36
rot 71
rub 35
rubber 21
rude 87
rummage 117
run along 19
run over 164
runt 18, 140
runty 19
rush 38, 140
rust 34, 116

S

sac 131
sack 34
sag 120
sail 94
salutation 58, 184
satisfaction 182
scamper 138
scatter 152
scheme 62, 151
scold 68
scoop 93, 182
scramble 83, 145
scrap 29, 46
scrape 47
scraping 46

scratch 20, 92, 119
scrub 134
scruple 70
scum 98
scuttle 95
scythe 33
seasoned 158
secure 172
sedentary 86
seize 84
sensational 111
sentiment 173
sermon 104
shade 36
share 96
shave 105, 135
shed 37, 145
sheepfold 33
shell 69
shift 125
shine 20
shove 140
Shredded Wheat 45
shriek 18
shrill 182
shrink 118
sideboard 147
sigh 85, 125
signal 56
silky 147
silly 58
sincere 69
sink 19
skim milk 45, 145

skip 39
slam 87
slant 48
slap 95
slat 138
sled 180
slight 88
slingshot 78
slip 22
slogan 108
slop 38, 57, 110
smoked 158
smudge 135
snap 75, 124, 161
snare 114
snarl 71, 158
sneak 38
sneaker 18
sneer 151, 182
sniff 35, 86, 180
snip 175
snooze 99
snout 27, 115, 166
soak 50, 168
soapy 93
sob 173
sociable 125
sod 36
solemn 103, 175
solid 104
sonny 47
sop 18
sorrow 173
sour 49

spang 103
sparrow 67, 152
spatter 44
specimen 20
spend 144
spike 117
spill 136
spinneret 83, 173
spit 68
splash 28, 93, 168
spoil 57, 130
spool 176
spotless 166
spread 104
spring 39
sprinkling 144
spruce 184
spy 49
squash 139, 180
squeal 183
squeeze 35
stableboy 159
stairway 48
stale 46, 85, 98
stalk 68
stall 32
starry 150
starve 86
stealthy 49
steer 144
stem 68, 124
stick 78
sticky 28, 114
stiff 66

stink 71, 95
stir 38, 152
stirring 54
stomach 41
stool 34, 74
stopper 117
storyteller 124
stove 19
stowaway 139
straddle 94
strain 172
strand 82, 102, 157, 180
straw 26, 134
streaky 182
stream 119
stretch 58
stretch out 147
strip 35
stroke 26, 165
stroll 36
struggle 139
stuck up 130
stuff 159
stunt 131
succeed 95
suck 21, 78
suggest 95
suitable 166
sulphur 50
summer squash 98
summon 85, 176
sunstroke 141
supernatural 166
supper 46

suppertime 26
supreme 108
surpass 138
surrounding 87
suspicious 159
swallow 34, 89
swamp 67
swathe 66
sway 84
sweet pea 87
swell 115
swing 93, 134
swish 97
swollen 146
swoop 68, 119
swoosh 97

T

tackle 119
tag along 28
tailgate 140, 164
tan 183
tangle 59, 119
tap 40
tarsus 82
task 114
tatter 116
tear 109
tease 135
teeter 67
terrific 109, 166
thee 151
thermometer 181
this instant 140

thistle 44
thorough 56
thrash 119, 141, 173
thread 59, 99, 176
throw in 74
thrush 121
thrust 88
thud 85
thump 84
thunder 66
tibia 82
tickle 169
tie-up 33, 115
timothy 67
tin 116
tinkle 71
tiny 21
toasty 47
tobacco 87
token 167
tongue 94
topmost 161
topple 95
toss 140, 174
touching 175
tough 156
trail 85, 183
trailer 176
trample 136
tranquil 186
trap 60
treasure 137, 185
tree toad 87
tremble 88, 183

tremendous 172
trench 45
trickle 135, 160
trifle 172
trill 87
trinket 181
triumph 165
triumphant 118
trochanter 82
trot 86, 136
trough 35, 88
troupe 88
trousers 169
trout 66
truffle 86
trust 34
tube 114
tuck 55, 153
turnip 181
tussle 139
.22 75
twilight 87
twirl 36, 48
twitch 131

U
unable 160
unattractive 146
unbearable 96
unconscious 167
underneath 50
unfair 18
unique 165
unremitting 69
untenable 71
unusual 103
updraft 184
uphill 39
upsidedown 47
utter 103

V
vague 78, 124
van 176
vanish 27, 152
veil 102
veritable 137
versatile 131
victim 74
vine 69

W
waddle 58
wade 28
wag 67
wagon 67
wander 34, 92
wasp 127
waterproof 156, 176
weakling 19
weary 146, 160
weather-vane 55
weave 82
weed 38, 68
weep 29
wheat 40
whence 166
whippoorwill 87
whisker 48, 96, 110, 157
whisper 20, 55, 103, 153
whistle 88
willing 85
wipe out 61
wisecrack 175
wit 61
witness 82
wobble 20
wonder 79
wondrous 104
woodchuck 182
woodpecker 48
woodshed 26, 115, 135
worm 69
wormy 151
worth 41
wrapper 46
writhe 119

Y
yard 26
yarn 138
yawn 55, 174
yell 18, 160

Z
zoom 94

🐔 영어원서 읽기 Tips

Charlotte's Web을 완독하셨군요! 축하합니다!

원서 읽는 단어장을 활용해보세요!

다양한 원서들을 「원서 읽는 단어장」을 활용해서 읽어보세요. 원서 읽는 단어장은 〈Charlotte's Web〉 외에도 〈Charlie and the Chocolate Factory〉를 비롯한 로알드 달의 작품들과 〈Twilight〉, 〈Harry Potter and the Sorcerer's Stone〉 등 여러 영어원서의 단어장이 출간되어 있고 앞으로도 계속 출간될 예정입니다. 「원서 읽는 단어장」은 시중 서점 및 인터넷 서점에서 구입할 수 있습니다.

「원서 읽는 단어장」 시리즈
- Charlie and the Chocolate Factory
- Matilda
- James and the Giant Peach
- Shopaholic
- Frindle
- The Secret
- Twilight
- Harry Potter and the Sorcerer's Stone

인터넷 서점에서 '원서 읽는 단어장'을 검색해보세요!

함께 모여 원서 읽는 〈스피드 리딩 카페〉

함께 모여 원서를 읽는 〈스피드 리딩 카페 cafe.naver.com/readingtc〉를 방문해보세요. '수준별 추천 원서 목록', '함께 만든 원서별 단어장', '매월 진행되는 북클럽' 등 원서 읽기에 도움이 되는 자료가 넘쳐납니다. 무엇보다 원서를 함께 읽을 수천 명의 동료들을 만날 수 있는 멋진 곳입니다. 원서 읽기에 관심이 있으시다면 이곳을 방문해서 함께 참여해보세요!

영어원서 읽기 Tips

**많은 글을 읽는 것은 영어를 익히는 가장 좋은 방법이 아니다.
그것은 '유일한' 방법이다.** – 세계적인 언어학자 스티븐 크라센 교수

영어원서 읽기는 모두가 인정하는 최고의 영어 공부법입니다. 일상에서 영어를 사용하지 않는 비영어권 국가에서 영어에 가장 쉽고, 편하고, 저렴하게 노출되는 방법이 '원서 읽기'이기 때문입니다. 하지만 영어 구사력이 뛰어나지 않은 한국의 보통 영어 학습자들에게는 선뜻 시작하기 부담스러운 것도 사실입니다.

이런 학습자들을 위하여 영어 초보자들도 쉽게 원서 읽기를 시작하고, 꾸준한 읽기를 통해 '영어원서 읽기 습관'을 만들 수 있도록 고안된 책을 소개합니다.

한국인을 위한 맞춤형 영어원서, '영화로 읽는 영어원서'

「영화로 읽는 영어원서」시리즈는 유명 영화를 기반으로 한 소설판 영어원서로, 내용 이해와 영어실력 향상을 위한 다양한 콘텐츠가 덧붙여져 있어 보다 쉽고 부담 없이 원서 읽기를 시작할 수 있습니다. 또한 리스닝과 영어 낭독 훈련에 도움이 되는 오디오북까지 함께 제공하여 원서를 부담 없이 읽으면서 자연스럽게 영어실력이 향상되도록 도와줍니다.

영화로 읽는 영어원서 시리즈 도서 목록

- 각 도서는 해당 영화의 소설판 영어원서입니다.

WALL-E
2008년 픽사 애니메이션
WALL-E

UP
2009년 픽사 애니메이션
UP

HIGH SCHOOL MUSICAL 1~3
디즈니 뮤지컬 무비 HIGH SCHOOL MUSICAL

THE PRINCESS AND THE FROG
2010년 디즈니 애니메이션
THE PRINCESS AND THE FROG

A CHRISTMAS CAROL
2009년 로버트 저메키스 제작 3D 애니메이션
A CHRISTMAS CAROL

ALICE IN WONDERLAND
2010년 팀 버튼 감독 3D 무비
ALICE IN WONDERLAND

출간된 본 시리즈 도서들은 독자들의 큰 사랑을 받으며 어학 분야의 베스트셀러를 기록했고, 학원과 학교들에서도 꾸준히 교재로 채택되는 등 영어 학습자들에게 좋은 반응을 얻고 있습니다. (EBS가 운영하는 어학 사이트 EBSlang(www.ebslang.co.kr), 서초·강남 등지 명문 중고교 방과 후 보충 교재 채택 등)

Text copyright © 2010 Longtail Books

원서읽는 단어장

Charlotte's Web

1판 1쇄 2010년 4월 12일
1판 18쇄 2025년 6월 9일

기획 이수영
책임편집 김수진 유난영
콘텐츠제작 롱테일 교육 연구소
마케팅 두잉글 사업본부

펴낸이 이수영
펴낸곳 롱테일북스
출판등록 제2015-000191호
주소 04033 서울특별시 마포구 양화로 113, 3층(서교동, 순흥빌딩)
전자메일 help@ltinc.net

ISBN 978-89-5605-451-3 14740
      978-89-5605-319-6 (세트)